PRAISE FOR 'WIN, WIN, WIN!'

'I loved reading this book. For me, surprisingly so, as I thought to myself, "How much new news can really be said on this topic?" But I loved it. It is extremely well-written, easy to digest and with lots of humour. More importantly, however, is the fact that it makes you reflect on all those cases where outcomes could have been better—for you, for your adversary and for both parties together. Philip Waterhouse simply does not accept the potential "lose" outcomes of the original Win-Win model and proposes new ways and a new, interesting model to look at business relationships. Hence, there is also a vibrant, optimistic can-do/will-do spirit that exudes from every page. That gave me energy when reading the book, and I did so with a smile on my face. Recommended!'
Poul Skadhede, Group CEO, Valcon Business Development A/S

'If Philip Waterhouse can't be on your team, then at least ensure your people have read this roadmap for winning. He speaks with the authority of a seasoned negotiator. His personal accounts of winning, and indeed losing, leave the reader in no doubt that his Win-Win-Win concept can bring incremental outcomes to the most challenging of situations. I was delighted by his refreshing philosophy, where integrity and engagement clearly trump even the most challenging adversaries. Waterhouse takes you back to the basics—understanding the other side's P&L for example—and then on a journey that dovetails a wide array of real-life situations that bring his new dimension to Win-Win—the Mutual Win—to life. This is a book for everyone in business—whether you are negotiating your next pay rise or a multi-million-dollar sales initiative on a new continent.'
Tom Chadwick, CEO GI Energy

'Responsible companies have long understood that a Win-Win approach to negotiations makes business sense. The most enlightened have also realized that the best Win-Win outcome includes the wider stakeholder community winning too. As companies have to think about their societal impact more than ever, in this important new book, Philip Waterhouse adds a new winning dimension that explains, together with practical examples, how negotiators can now achieve even better winning solutions for their companies.'

Duncan Edwards, CEO Britishamerican Business,
ex-president & CEO Hearst Magazines International

'Philip Waterhouse presents a key strategic approach to unlocking growth in any organisation. Although I would agree with him that professional pride is important, what shines throughout this book is strategic leadership underpinned by empathy, a key differentiator for any organisation's future. The events of 2020 have clarified the fragility of supply chains, organisations and even nations, which now require new leadership strategies. I strongly recommend that this Win-Win-Win method is added to your strategic tool kit, now. Why? The future of business is not competitive but collaborative, as technology drives change at a societal level, with speed.'

Dr. Jacqui Taylor, CEO Flyingbinary,
expert advisor to the United Nations,
G20, European Commission and the UK government

'There is an art and a science to negotiating effectively, and Philip Waterhouse's book straddles both really well. But what I like best about the book is the way Waterhouse takes his disruptive new model, based on the Mutual Win, and weaves it into a series of case studies, based on real-life scenarios that bring his new model to life. It will be of interest to many of us in business. *Win, Win, Win!* is a practical, methodical, grounded-in-real-life book that business professionals will engage with, written concisely and with humour. I seriously recommend *Win, Win, Win!* to anyone who has to negotiate as a manager, a leader or a professional. So that makes all of us!'

Jeremy Cassell, coach, trainer and co-author of bestselling
books 'Brilliant Selling' and 'The Leader's Guide to Presenting'

'Following many years of a successful business journey, Waterhouse's book is much more than just a "give-back" exercise. It demonstrates a genuine sense of generosity and gratitude, the glues that bind people together as the enablers and accelerators of success. Page after page, you discover that there is no Win-Win without these enablers. *Win, Win, Win!* is a MUST-READ!'
Jacques Amey, partner, Heidrick & Struggles

'In *Win, Win, Win!*, Philip Waterhouse has laid out a cogent way for leaders to develop the mind-set to create a mutual win in negotiations. He invokes the important topic of conscience and, with a multitude of stories and case studies, shows the way to diffuse—even overturn— those perennially confrontational business relationships. A worthy read for anyone who wants to improve their negotiation results.'
Minter Dial, professional speaker and the author of 'You Lead: How Being Yourself Makes You a Better Leader', the award-winning 'Heartificial Empathy' and 'The Last Ring Home'

'When the world we're operating in is made all the more challenging by complexity and ambiguity, our ability to connect with clients and colleagues gets tested to the max. Developing this differentiating competency has perhaps never been more mission-critical. Philip Waterhouse provides insights, strategies and a tried-and-tested model that can help take the strain. Couple that with a writing style that enables the reader to navigate a path to the change they seek, and you know you have in your hands a practical game changer. Buy it! Read it!'
Jim Steele, business speaker, leadership facilitator and coach

'Based on extensive management experience, real case studies and best-practice reflection, *Win, Win, Win!* is a must-read for anyone looking to improve their negotiation skills and business acumen.'
Chris Garthwaite, CEO, CGA Experience

First published in 2021.

ISBNs
Paperback   978-2-9577700-0-7
E-book   978-2-9577700-1-4

Library of Congress Cataloging-in-Publication Data
Name: Waterhouse, Philip
Title: Win, Win, Win! A New Dimension In Winning In Your Business / Philip Waterhouse
BISAC Code: Business & Economics : Leadership / Negotiating / Personal Success
Cover Design: Tom Howey
Book Layout: Jovana Lukic

Note that any page cross references refer to the print edition

WIN, WIN, WIN!

A New Dimension to Winning in Your Business

Philip Waterhouse

TABLE OF CONTENTS

PART 3
WIN-WIN-WIN IN YOUR BUSINESS

PART 4
CONCLUSION

ACKNOWLEDGEMENTS

I am not a writer by trade. I am just passionate about this topic. I would therefore like to thank all those people that have either contributed or helped me put this book together.

First, I would like to warmly express my gratitude to Minter Dial and Jeremy Cassell, two accomplished authors who unselfishly gave me their top tips on how to go about this task, and to my case-study inspirations (in alphabetical order)—Laurent Guillaume, Pierre Jacquot, Robert Jervis, Hervé Legrand, Didier Voire and Cédric Wehry.

I would also like to thank my wife, Valérie, and three children, Léa, Iona and Oscar, who put up with me during the writing process. Not an easy task!

Thanks too to my editor, Sophie Miodownik, for scrubbing up the book, Jovana Lukić for the perfect formatting, and Tom Howey for such an impactful book cover.

And last but by no means least... I must thank my mother, who waded through my first draft and has always been a great support to me in endeavours such as this!

EARNING THE RIGHT

Nearly 25 years ago, I was appointed managing director of a world-leading haircare brand. The brand had three key values that had to be applied at the start of any presentation to an audience you have never presented to before.

One of the values was that it was necessary to 'earn the right' to be listened to by an audience, particularly a new one. This applied to every employee, no matter the number of stripes on your sleeve.

If you did not earn the right, your audience had no necessary reason to listen to you and thereby take on board what you had to say. It was a question of respect to your audience.

I have adhered to this notion at every presentation to an audience I don't know since then (and would recommend it to you, too, in your own professional life). It is a simple exercise in courtesy, humility and transparency.

Presenting to an unfamiliar reader is no different. So, allow me to do so now.

As an undergraduate I specialized in Mathematics, and a few years into my professional career I stepped back and took a Masters in Business Administration (MBA) degree. Since then, I have gained more than 30 years of experience in the world of consumer goods—across 4 continents; in over 12 countries; within virtually every single consumer-goods channel that has ever been invented, from wholesale to retail. I have worked in several different sectors, in stock-exchange quoted and family-owned companies of different origins and with very different company cultures.

My last 25 years of experience have been in general management leadership roles, with full profit and loss (P&L) statement accountability, with either national or regional responsibility. These rich experiences have business transformation as their common denominator.

This broad experience has brought me nose-to-nose with the concept of Win-Win on virtually a daily basis across all the business functions.

Win-Win has been my guiding light over these 25 years. It has not been just a negotiation technique. It has been one of my personal values that have made me successful (in my own modest way).

Accordingly, if you are looking to be successful in your career, potentially in a senior leadership role, in any company, no matter the size (turnover, profit or people), and believe that Win-Win will be one of the key success factors to get you there, please read on.

If you are reading this book to get the top tips on becoming the CEO of a worldwide Fortune 500, Nasdaq, FTSE 100 or CAC 40 company, then I hope you kept the receipt. This will not be the book for you. It is not the objective of the book.

I am not an academic. This book is about the front line—not the lecture theatre or focus groups. It is based on hands-on experience. Not a questionnaire. Not classroom theory, nor strategic-consultancy PowerPoint presentations either.

I am not a devourer of business literature, although this book clearly is about business. I do not believe (perhaps foolishly) that knowing the personal insights of a one-in-a-gazillion CEO will make me successful as a leader from tomorrow. Although I am sure that their books would make an interesting read.

However, I do believe that business literature should help anyone like you or me successfully manage the professional milestones that we have to take in order to climb each step of the professional ladder successfully. By their very nature, these professional milestones will take you out of your comfort zone.

For each of these milestones, best-practice business books can provide bull's-eye insights and a welcome professional support in best practices to help you navigate your way.

There are a few professional milestones that spring to mind.

- <u>Taking on a New Role</u> in a new sector or company. I thoroughly recommend *The First 90 Days* by Michael Watkins (Gildan Media). A must-read book if you ever take on a new role way outside your comfort zone!
- <u>Managing Conflict</u>. *Resolving Conflicts at Work* by Kenneth Cloke and Joan Goldsmith (Jossey-Bass) was a very useful guide to me.
- Making an impact to others through your <u>Communication and Presentation Skills</u>. I thoroughly enjoyed *The Leader's Guide to Presenting* by Tom Bird and Jeremy Cassell (Financial Times Publishing).
- <u>Hitting the Ground Running in a New Business Discipline</u>, such as moving from finance to supply chain, from sales to marketing (or vice versa). No book recommendations here. The topic is too vast. It depends on where you've come from and where you are moving to.

Believing in Win-Win is, as far as I am concerned, one of these professional milestones.

I learnt this from *doing*. I am writing this book to help you complement your own doing with a process, a series of best practices and maybe new ideas to help you get there faster. After all, and assuming you want to be successful (i.e.

win), you will not get there by yourself. You will only get there by bringing your stakeholders, internal or external, on board.

I won't embarrass you by saying that they will not participate in your winning if there is nothing in it for them. They need to win somewhere along the way, too.

In this respect, Win (you)–Win (them) is the quickest, if not only, sure way to the success that you aspire to. This book brings a new, additional Win (both of you) dimension to the table.

My objective is to help you to get there: Win-Win-Win!

I humbly appreciate that I am not the first person to write about winning. Indeed, as I start to write this book, there are over 1200 titles that I could buy on Amazon (in English) with the word *win* in the title! I have not, and will not pretend, that I have researched each and every one of them to put my own book together on what I call this new dimension in winning.

I hope that I have earned the right for you to read on and learn more.

Before you kick off with the book, I have three other housekeeping topics I would like to share with you.

- In this book I will refer a great deal to the Win-Win Matrix. It is frankly the best tool that there is to help capture the stakes in any subject matter where winning and losing are in the balance. It is visually simple to understand and is composed of a square split equally into four boxes, or quadrants (see Figure 0.1) across vertical and horizontal axes. Like any graph, the idea is that a 'more' or 'less' position can be plotted on each of the two axes.
- While the outcomes of each quadrant never change, there are several different interpretations of the X- and Y-axes. Among others, I have seen 'relationship' and

'issue'[1]; 'courage' and 'consideration'[2]; 'focus on our objectives' and 'focus on their objectives'[3]; 'benefits to you and 'benefits to others'[4]; 'focus on your own needs' and 'focus on the other's needs'[5]. We can conclude that there is no golden rule for the axes, although the spirit is the same. Each reference to the Win-Win Matrix appears to have adapted the axes' names according to the author's objective in the article in question.

I shall therefore do the same, not only when referring to the Win-Win Matrix, but also to my own, new model that I will introduce in Part 2, for the sake of consistency and to enable comparison between the two models. I believe that the X- and Y-axes represents the two stakeholders in any negotiation, namely you and your Adversary. This relationship can be summarized by the relative position to the other—*strong* or *weak*. Appreciation of this comes, of course, by comparing your position to that of your Adversary. Am I stronger than my Adversary? Is my Adversary stronger than I? But it also comes by understanding how strong your business situation is *per se*. This strength (or weakness) can be assessed by innumerable criteria that we will dig into in more detail in the book. The same goes for your Adversary's business.

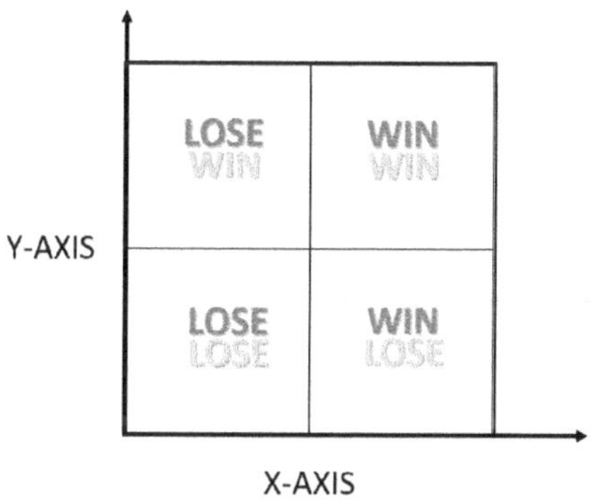

Figure 0.1 – Win-Win Matrix

- In order to give an extra little standout, but without wanting to ruffle the feathers of grammatical sticklers, I will always pick out in capital letters the key words that are part and parcel of the Win-Win topic and the book. For instance, Win, Lose, Adversary, etc.
- Lastly, I will respect the confidentiality of my case-study contributors by changing the protagonists' names (except for one, at their request!) and never mentioning names of the companies. I trust that this will be an issue for no one. The objective of each of the case studies is to highlight the issues at stake, rather than the specific details of whoever or wherever.

On the basis that none of these are insurmountable issues, you are good to go!

By the way, this is my first book. The stakes are high for me too. Now you know that I have something to win too!

Enjoy.

A WINNING INTRODUCTION

For more than 50 years, the term Win-Win has been used in both professional and personal contexts to describe the best way, the ideal way, to resolve conflict.

Today, world leaders, such as former president Donald Trump, use the term Win-Win when referring to complex geopolitical negotiations. So when it comes to a negotiation, Win-Win has become a recognized household term. Indeed, the power of the term Win-Win is that it needs no dictionary definition to be understood. We do not need any explanation to understand the interest of a Win-Win outcome to any negotiation.

It's simple. You win. I win.

That easy. Job done.

But my view is that there is more to Win-Win than the self-evident outcome to any negotiation. I believe that, in a business context, Win-Win is a value. Win-Win is a personal compass that should guide executives in their everyday business lives and behaviour. It is about the respect you have for your team and/or employees. It is the respect that you have for your suppliers, your customers and your competitors, too. In fact, everyone.

To capture this, the conventional notion of Win-Win needs an extra dimension. This third, extra dimension is the 'everyone' part. The 'we', together. Put simply, the third mutual Win.

Win-Win-Win.

By adding this dimension, I will demonstrate to you the additional wins, the more uplifting wins—perhaps the ones that you haven't thought of—in all your business negotiations both externally, to suppliers and customers, and internally to stakeholders within your business, above and below.

It is this third Win dimension that is the game changer.

The book is split into four parts.

In Part 1, I will explore where Win-Win started and where it has taken us up to today. We will look at the traditional model that is used to help us navigate through Win-Win—the Win-Win Matrix—and examine each of its four predicted outcomes. Finally, we will explore the pros and cons of this Win-Win Matrix as a means of *walking the walk* and *talking the talk* of Win-Win.

In Part 2, I will add the third dimension and a new model, the Win-Win-Win Pyramid. The third Win. I will explain how the third Win is the key to unlocking the other two. It is important to understand how the third Win complements the other two. This third Win will ensure that no matter the conventional outcome of the Win-Win Matrix, you will always end up with a better outcome than before. A worthy cause, I hope you agree.

We will then cover how to bring your Adversary to the Win-Win table even if, at first glance, they appear uninterested.

Lastly, we will also look at other important topics around Win-Win such as category management, how to prepare for your negotiation and (yes) losing.

Part 3 is more practical. More hands on. We will apply Win-Win-Win to multiple business scenarios, thanks to a series of case studies. It cannot be, and will not be, an exhaustive set of examples, but I hope to give you a broad framework to apply to your business. In each of these case studies, we will examine real-life Win-Win situations in order to stimulate you as to how what we have covered can help you in your business.

To help you navigate through the book, each chapter in Parts 1 and 2 will start with what you should expect to take away from the chapter.

In Part 3, on the other hand, at the end of each case study, we will look 'beyond the case' to demonstrate its broader relevance to businesses in other sectors, or of different sizes.

As you read these case studies, I ask you to consider a relevant example for your business and work through what you might have learnt.

As an exercise, give one of your direct reports the task to work on the same example at the same time. Trust me, if the example is genuinely relevant, it will be a worthy exercise. As with all important tasks, two brains will produce a better outcome than one. Make the example the subject of your next one-on-one with this person.

Certain chapters in Part 3 might be more relevant to you in your business. If this is the case, spend more time on these and skim others that you believe less relevant.

That said, if, like me, Win-Win (and now a third Win) is part of your intrinsic business ethic, I am sure you will find each case study worth reading.

Finally, in Part 4, we will pull all the pieces together into a tight conclusion.

And then you're done.

Before we get stuck in, and in order for you to use this book as a practical game changer, I would like to start you off with a challenge.

Think of your worst personal case study, one where you always stand to lose, or you have always lost. You know, the one that gives you sleepless nights and more stress than you would care to deal with.

It might be the one where you have always had to give significant discount concessions to maintain your so-called business partnership. Or, the one where every time your Adversary invents another non-negotiable reason why you have to lower your prices and reduce significantly your profitability. Or, the one where no matter what you say, the only language they understand is 'I win. You lose'.

If you need to, write down the following things. I'll let you get a pen and paper...

Let's call this personal case study the Nightmare. Start with a few simple questions:
- Why is the Nightmare a nightmare?
- What are you losing? Why?
- What are the levers, in or out of the box, that will help you lose less? Remember that even from the moment when you start to lose less you are kind of winning. You are on the right path!
- What quantitative or qualitative arguments can you think of that might put you on this right path?

Put these questions in a safe place and keep reading.

As you read through this book, keep the Nightmare in mind and, if you like, constantly refer back to it as you work through the chapters to see whether the book helps give you some pointers on the next Nightmare negotiation or interaction you will have.

My objective is that it will.

If we make progress on the Nightmare, you will then be able to move on to your next shocker of a personal case study (let's call it the Bad Dream!) and so on and so on.

PART 1

WIN-WIN

THE ORIGINS AND SCOPE OF WIN-WIN

Key Takeaways

> 1. There are seven business, economic and social cases where Win-Win applies.
> 2. Win-Win was first coined in the context of human relationships, not in a business context.
> 3. Win-Win applies to all businesses. Without exception.

In all forms of contest, it is to be expected that if one party wins, the other party loses. Win-Lose.

So, in its most basic form, the notion of Win-Win is to demonstrate that there is an alternative outcome than this traditional and well-understood one.

In a corporate context, John Stacey[1]—in his article 'Seven Examples of Win Win'—tells us where Win-Win applies.

Negotiation: In business, negotiations take place on a daily basis. Sometimes several times a day. A Win-Win negotiation is one between two parties where both end up with an outcome that they believe can be beneficial to them.

For instance, let's say one party from Company X has negotiated a favourable price for a product from another party from Company Y. Company X appears to have won. But to secure this price, Company X has agreed to buy a new, additional product from Company Y. So, too, has Company Y.

Accordingly, both parties take away something from the negotiation.

Strategy: A company is developing a new technology, which they believe can become the industry standard going forward. They believe that their winning hand is to ensure that they make the technology available to every player in the market, including competitors. They believe that, by doing so, they will have a competitive advantage that goes beyond this new technology.

Leadership: A Win-Win leader of a company, for instance, is one that surrounds him- or herself with first-class team members and develops them to their fullest potential. Such leaders understand the benefits of developing a strong network of loyal, talented individuals, where the collective outcome for the company is performance, and thereby results, that way exceed those of the company's competition. The consequent superior business performance means greater success for the leader.

Economy: At the economic level, a nation can achieve Win-Win that allows it to develop into, and thereby export, sectors that offer it a competitive advantage—while importing goods where it recognises it has a competitive disadvantage. Stacey gives us the example of a nation that is strong in the production of coffee, but poor at growing rice. This nation could strongly benefit from the exportation of coffee in return for the importation of rice, for instance.

Indeed, Win-Win has become a widespread term in contemporary geopolitics. China versus USA. Europe versus Brexit UK. Global economic interests versus those of the planet.

Games: A Win-Win game is one where there is no

Adversary to defeat. In such a game, the players of the game must come together and work as a team to complete the game.

Quality of Life: Quality-of-life improvements are often considered negative for the economy. To improve the air quality in a city, for instance, a city centre must be closed off to polluting vehicles. This, in turn, could well have a negative effect on the economy. This outcome does not necessarily have to be true. Stacey tells us that environmental regulations can spark new industries in areas such as clean energy, which develop new economic opportunities.

Another Win-Win example in this field is an increase to minimum wage. While it increases costs to companies, it can stimulate an increase in consumer spending and, thereby, the demand for their products.

Security: It is not necessarily true that in order for us all to feel, or be, more secure, we must give up our privacy. A Win-Lose. If we look at data technology, data encryption provides both data privacy and security. A Win-Win. Indeed, it can be strongly argued that streets are safer today, and crimes are more swiftly solved, thanks to closed-circuit cameras.

Given the significant economic scope for, and application of, Win-Win, one could expect that the term Win-Win was coined in a business context. It is not the case.

THE ORIGINS OF WIN-WIN

It is both interesting and, I believe, symbolic that the origin of the term Win-Win is in fact to be found in the context of human relationships.

In 1968, Dr. Victor Baranco founded Lafayette Morehouse in Lafayette, California. Lafayette Morehouse was an innovative community, where residents lived together in a group. Residents believed that group living best fitted human nature and led to a happier, more rewarding life experience.

Victor Baranco[2] believed that in order to sustain a cohesive group community, it was vital to handle communication, sensuality and decision-making. He coined the term Win-Win as a positive model for the group to make decisions on community life.

Of course, Victor Baranco was right.

The heart of Win-Win is human.

No matter the topic, a Win-Win outcome in any situation, on any level, can only happen if the humans behind the discussions want to make it happen. So humans, and thereby human relationships, are both the starting point and end point of any discussion in which Win-Win is on the table. If either party has no interest in the perspective of the other, then a Win-Win outcome becomes far more difficult to achieve.

The human aspect of Win-Win will be one of the major themes of this book. This book will not, however, look into the geopolitical uses and potential of Win-Win. It will focus on the application of Win-Win in business.

Win-Win success in business topics and the human relationships between Win-Win stakeholders are inter-related. You cannot have one without the other.

The notion of relationships between Win-Win stake-holders is perfectly illustrated in the image that is most often used to visualize what is meant by Win-Win.

In it, we see two donkeys strapped together by a rope. We see that by working together, not pulling against each other, they both eat their own bale of hay. Win-Win.

While the image is simple and compelling, it symbolizes this human component, or in this case donkey component, of cooperation and understanding to get to Win-Win. Their cooperation allowed them to get what they both wanted from the outset.

Figure 1.1.1 : Winning Donkeys[3]

I personally prefer another image, for which I can find neither a diagram nor an image, per se. Instead, let me share this with you in words.

Imagine two children who are fighting over an orange—the last one. They both want it. First, they fight over it. Of course. Then, one of the children has the foresight to ask why the other wants the orange in the first place.

The children discover that one of them wants the orange because they are thirsty, whilst the other one wants the orange to bake a cake. One wants the juice of the orange, the other wants the zest!

Thanks to the children having a mutual understanding of each other's needs, they can share the orange, and both achieve their objective. One can quench their thirst. The other will bake a cake.

As soon as they realise this, the fight stops. The child who wants to bake the cake takes the zest and then hands it to the other, who takes the juice.

Both of these examples are utopian views of Win-Win.

In both examples, we see the importance of communication. In the latter example, we see that both parties can ultimately share the same resource. This has particular resonance in a business context, as often the most difficult negotiations revolve specifically around the same resource—whether you're buying or selling a product, or buying or selling a service.

I want to buy it for less. You want to sell it for more.

It is utopian, in that all parties got exactly what they wanted in the first place. There is no more obvious example of a perfect Win-Win.

Business reality and experience demonstrates that the outcomes from most negotiations will, almost inevitably, involve a compromise of some sort. A discount or price compromise in a commercial contract. The rental value in a business lease. The price or service-level of a service agreement. The value or percentage in a bonus agreement.

The Rolling Stones[4] were not wrong. *You can't always get what you want.*

The scope of Win-Win, nonetheless, does not change. A Win-Win negotiation is one between two parties where both achieve an outcome that they believe can be beneficial to them.

So Win-Win applies to all businesses. No matter their business sector. No matter the business size. No matter the negotiation topic.

Win-Win applies both externally, between your business and someone else's, and internally, between different stakeholders within the same business.

Win-Win also applies to all business relationships and stakeholders.

Win-Win applies to all business functions. Sales, marketing, HR, supply chain... You name it.

So Win-Win can, and should, play a part in every dimension of the success you have in your professional role.

It could relate internally to the way you manage your own team members, or your boss. It could relate externally to the interactions you have with others outside the company.

This is why Win-Win is a topic that is worth taking seriously.

Let us dig deeper.

1.2

WHY SHOULD YOU BELIEVE IN WIN-WIN?

Key Takeaways

1. If you are not prepared to lose, consider Win-Win. Accept that Win-Win will mean some sort of compromise. It is neither black, nor white. It is inevitably a shade of grey.
2. Win-Lose invariably generates negative feelings for the losing party against the winning one.
3. Win-Lose can only go on for a finite time.

Let's face it, winning is better than losing.

Nobody wants to lose.

Karl Lagerfeld[1] famously said that 'Dieting is the only game where you win when you lose.'

So we can agree that we all believe, from a one-dimensional perspective, in Win!

But what about Win-Win? Win-Win is two-dimensional.

It brings your Adversary into the equation and forces you to consider their position. Given that, for any specific event, we have just established that *you* want to win and *you* don't want to lose, it can be fair to say that your Adversary shares the same view.

Why Should You Believe in Win-Win?

If both parties go into an event, or negotiation, determined one-dimensionally to win and not to lose:
1. The event risks being pretty brutal, and
2. One of you is going to have to lose.

If this is not to be how the event plays out, then each party needs to consider the other. Each party needs to understand what Win looks like. And what Lose looks like.

If Win is black, then Lose must be white.

Believing in Win-Win means accepting that Win cannot be black, as it forces Lose to be white.

Instead, believing in Win-Win is to understand that Win is some sort of shade of grey. For both of you.

In other words, you must identify, and agree to, a greyer-than-black outcome that looks like a Win to you—which, viewed from your Adversary's perspective, is a greyer-than-white outcome that does not mean Lose to them. In the business context of Win-Win, this event is invariably a negotiation.

In business, negotiations happen on a daily basis. It is unrealistic to accept that, over a full career in business, you will win every one of them. Inevitably you will lose some.

This should not dent your belief in Win-Win. Win-Win is both short-term (e.g. the, or a, specific negotiation) and long-term.

By believing, understanding, and accepting what this grey Win looks like, you will gain a chance of winning more often.

Believing in Win-Win means you understand that:
- It's all about more than one single event, negotiation or action.
- You are prepared to understand what the different versions of Win could look like.
- You will aim to understand, each time, the position of your Adversary.

Win-Lose also has human consequences. Losing emotions are bitterness, disappointment, resentment, frustration, to mention just a few printable ones! None are positive.

When two Adversaries strike a Win-Win deal, they will have fundamentally completely different feelings towards one another than two Adversaries where one of the parties has unequivocally lost.

If these two same Adversaries have to conduct another negotiation, then the going-in anticipation will be more positive and optimistic if the outcome of the last one was Win-Win.

Alternatively, in this second negotiation, if one of the parties loses for a second time, these negative emotions are further accentuated. The relationship, not to mention the partnership between the two companies, will deteriorate further.

Keep going like this, and there will be only a finite amount of time before the losing party will throw in the towel or ask for the parameters of the business relationship to be completely renegotiated.

For the repeatedly winning party, if the repeatedly losing Adversary is a major stakeholder in a key supplier/customer relationship, there is a risk of rupture. A new supplier/customer for similar products/services will have to be found... at the same price... and in a timescale that might not be of your deciding.

Let me share with you a personal experience to illustrate the point. I worked in a senior leadership role at a women's fashion brand for a number of years.

A few years into my role, I set up a lunch with my peer at a men's fashion brand who worked with independent (i.e. small owner-driver businesses) customers of a similar profile to mine. While my company sold to customers targeting women, my peer sold to those targeting men. We met to discuss best practices and compare notes on the state of the distribution channel.

While my business was strong and progressing (albeit not at the pace that I would have liked), their business was not... at all.

It turned out that the men's brand had used its dominant position with their customers to impose excessive commercial conditions over a number of seasons—spring/summer and autumn/winter.

At first, this policy had brought high rewards, but by the end of several seasons, their customers started to fall by the wayside. They went out of business. They simply couldn't afford the Win-Lose terms imposed by the men's brand and they couldn't find an equally strong brand as an alternative.

In short, my peer had to admit that their short-term, season-by-season, Win-Lose strategy ended in a resounding Lose-Lose. Their distribution base disintegrated like melting snow. Both parties ended up losing. Unfortunately, there was no second chance.

Believing in Win-Win not only has short-term tangible, financial benefits, event by event, but also longer-term ones. The same is true on a human relationship level.

In my experience, business partnerships of all kinds are made up of what is stated in the contract, and then what is *not* stated. What is *not* stated will be on top of contractual terms, by definition.

What is *not* stated can be genuinely unexpected events or circumstances; unforeseen requests or topics that are decided by senior management, non-negotiable internally and so pushed down (or across) the business; new projects or ideas that were not on the discussion table at the time of the contract. The scope for what is *not* stated is endless.

It is clear that your partners will be more inclined to support you on the on tops in the event that you are in a Win-Win partnership than one where you are resented because you insist, or thrive, on Win-Lose.

Once you believe in Win-Win, it becomes a way of being. It becomes a state of mind. A principle that defines the way you do business. Used on a daily basis, it can be one of the key contributors to making you and your business successful.

Once you believe in Win-Win, one of the key challenges is to understand what grey looks like. There will be no black and there should be no white. This is not necessarily a straightforward task.

If you take a commercial supplier/customer relationship, this grey task will require an (ideally in-depth) understanding of your business, the business's profit and loss statement that is under your responsibility and the interactions between each of the lines.

Is Win maximizing turnover? Is Win maximizing profitability? If it is profitability, is it profit in absolute value or percentage?

Is Win maximizing market share?

Are there other parameters to Win, such as service levels? Payment terms? Product- or category-based?

If you take an employee remuneration scheme, for instance, it will require an in-depth understanding of:
- The business's human capital
- The interaction between each function and organization level
- A lucid appreciation of the interests of each employee group versus those of the total business
- ...and so on.

Understanding your Adversary will be a topic we will look into in greater detail in Part 2.

Lastly, while I am advocating that believing in Win-Win is way of working on a journey towards success, I am not suggesting that it is the only way to become successful.

There are many successful people in business, and successful businesses, that have clearly achieved financial success simply believing in a one-dimensional win. They win. All others lose, no matter their relationship with them or their business!

Fair enough, and well done indeed to them. That said, their path to this financial success cannot have been without human collateral damage—their own, or that of their Adversary, with whom they have interacted to help them get there. That must stay on their conscience.

1.3

THE WIN-WIN MATRIX

Key Takeaways

1. The Win-Win Matrix indicates that there are four probable outcomes of any negotiation, based on your relative position of strength to your Adversary.
2. In three quadrants out of four, the Win-Win Matrix suggests that one party, including yourself, should expect to lose.
3. Where both you and your Adversary are relatively weak, the Win-Win Matrix suggests that both parties should lose. A more optimistic Win-Win approach would be to imply that both parties can still win, albeit on a lower scale due your respectively weak situations.

The most popular tool for predicting an outcome of a negotiation is the Win-Win Matrix.

The Win-Win Matrix is a visual representation of the potential, or probable, outcome of an interaction between yourself and a third party—your Adversary—based on your relative positions of strength or weakness versus one another.

The Win-Win Matrix

The idea behind the Win-Win Matrix is that you first plot your own position relative to your Adversary on a scale of weakness to strength.

There are several criteria that can help you decide if ultimately you are in a weak or strong negotiating position.

Such criteria might be:
- Your company size versus theirs
- The market share of your product or service in your Adversary's business
- Your competitive position in your market. Are there several other competitors who offer the same, or similar, products or services?
- Your business's financial solidity. What could be the consequences to your business if you lose in this negotiation?
- What are the key areas where you could lose and how important to you are these areas?
- Will there be knock-on effects on other parts of the business if you lose?

Figure 1.3.1 : Traditional Representation of Win-Win Matrix

- The longevity, and quality, of your relationship
- The recent history of your relationship—your recent collaborations, your service levels achievements. Have you been delivering against your promises? Have they been delivering against their promises?
- The current market dynamics. Is the market growing or declining?
- Your company's current financial situation. How well is the company doing—turnover, profitability, market share?
- Have there been any on-top events that you have responded favourably or unfavourably to?
- … and so on.

There is no exact science that will help you plot exactly where you and your Adversary are on each of the two axes. You just have to take a view. It is your view.

Once your relative positions have been plotted using the Win-Win Matrix, the Matrix gives you an indication of the potential, probable, or predicted outcome.

In a nutshell, you win or lose. Ditto for your Adversary.

While somewhat simplistic, of course, this exercise of plotting positions on the Matrix is very useful. It forces you to consider multiple variables and look at all aspects of the topic before you enter into the field of play. The more time and criteria you take into consideration, not only will you have a more accurate view of your relative positions, but also you will be prepared for the upcoming action.

It goes without saying that the best place to be is one where your position is strong. According to the Win-Win Matrix, you hold a winning hand. Likewise, you want to avoid being in a position of weakness. Here, your hand is not good.

The Win-Win Matrix identifies four different outcomes.

WIN-WIN

Both hands are strong; the situation is balanced.

In the Win-Win quadrant, we see that both parties can achieve a positive outcome. For instance:

1. A *product negotiation*, where a supplier accepts a lower purchase price, but based on agreed guaranteed increases in volume that generate a commensurate lower production cost to manufacture. Both parties should see an equal increase in profitability.
2. A new *service agreement*, where the service provider lowers the price of Service A in return for the customer taking on a new (and more profitable) Service B.
3. A *union negotiation*, where an employer accepts a new profit-sharing scheme for employees, based on mutually beneficial profit or turnover targets.
4. A *store-rent agreement* between retailer and property owner, where rental payments are reduced based on mutually beneficial shop turnover targets.

In all of these examples, both parties agree on an outcome in which they are each better off financially.

In addition, on a human level, both parties (most probably) come out of the discussions with mutual respect and a closer partnership going forward.

WIN-LOSE OR LOSE-WIN

Either: The situation is in your favour; your situation is stronger than that of your Adversary.

Or: The situation is not in your favour; your situation is weaker than that of your Adversary.

In each of these two quadrants, there is a winner and a loser. Let us take the same four examples as above. Our outcomes change.

1. In the *price negotiation*, where a supplier has no choice but to accept the price reduction, based on the same volume, such that one of the two parties imposes their will on the other.
2. In the *service agreement*, where the service provider must reluctantly agree to reduce the price of Service A. Your Adversary, or you, simply refuse to consider Service B. There will be no trade.
3. The *union negotiation* with the employer does not result in any profit-sharing scheme. There will be no negotiation on topics that might be mutually beneficial.
4. In the *rent agreement*, there is no opportunity to reduce rental payments, no matter the shop turnover. Take it or leave it.

One winner. One loser.

What is common between these different examples is the human aspect.

While the winner may, or may not, be elated with their win, it is virtually guaranteed that the loser is not satisfied with their loss. Sooner or later, this dissatisfaction can lead to resentment or disrespect vis-à-vis their Adversary.

In the Win-Lose or Lose-Win quadrants, both the financial and human outcomes will inevitably jeopardise the longevity of the collaboration.

LOSE-LOSE

Let us also focus on this bottom-left category, where both hands are weak. The situation is balanced, as in the Win-Win quadrant.

The Win-Win Matrix indicates that both parties lose. At face value, the Lose-Lose quadrant is one where neither you nor your Adversary have the prospect of a positive outcome.

Traditionalists would advocate that in this scenario, the only strategy is to minimize the loss, rather than trying to find a win.

There are a few examples where a Lose-Lose outcome would appear to be the only option.

- A negotiation of a *divorce*, where significant legal fees cannot be avoided.
- A tragic *medical situation*, where the patient must decide to lose a limb if they are to have a chance of survival.
- A commercial *price war*—for instance, in the airline industry on a high-traffic route. On these routes, the price per seat for all competitors may go below the cost of providing the seat. This might be a choice, or it might be an imposition. The first competitor to increase their prices, even by a bit, risks losing significant volume. Here there is a danger of a vicious circle as all parties match each other in like-for-like price reductions. To make matters worse, or fair, competition law prevents all parties from getting around the table by colluding to exit the price war.
- A *project scenario*, if a contractor is overspending and thereby, potentially, looking for compensation from the client where the client benefit expectations for the project once launched are turning out lower than first anticipated.

These Lose-Lose scenarios do exist. They cannot be neglected or ignored. Nonetheless, they are the exception, not the rule.

That said, the objective in this bottom-left equally weak quadrant is to allow for alternative, better outcomes to prevail.

A Win-Win outcome, for instance? After all, both parties have the same relative position to one another.

This more optimistic outcome is dependent on the state of mind of the two parties. If both parties believe in Win-Win, then surely there is the opportunity for both parties to win.

Instead of a Lose-Lose outcome, let both parties envisage a Win-Win one. One where both parties enjoy some sort of a win, that is relevant, or scaled, to their relative positions of weakness as identified in the Win-Win Matrix.

For instance, if we compare this situation to the Win-Win quadrant, there is no reason why both parties cannot agree on the same outcome just because the quadrant position is different. In each case the financial amounts associated with the mutual win outcomes might be less significant, due to the weak position that both parties find themselves in. So be it.

For instance:

1. In the *product negotiation*, both parties could be in financial difficulties and recognize the fact that every cent of a price reduction is significant, and that alternatives to a higher/lower price should be explored.
2. In the *supplier agreement*, the price for Service A is marginally reduced and the price for Service B is marginally higher.
3. In the *union negotiation*, we see the same outcome as in the top-right Win-Win quadrant, but the values associated are lower for each party.
4. In the *rental agreement*, we see the same outcome but on a far more limited scale.

In other words, despite the relatively weak position of both parties they have managed to find an outcome that, at their level or scale, is nonetheless positive.

Additionally, on a human level, we are likely to see the same positive sentiments and mutual respect with regard to one another as in the top-right Win-Win quadrant.

Emotions, such as resentment and bitterness, are not expressed relative to the manner of the loss. They are principally based on the fact that you have Lost. You have not Won.

Accordingly, a more optimistic representation of the Win-Win Matrix looks like this (see *Figure 1.3.2*).

As a firm believer in Win-Win, I like it that this version is more aligned to the spirit of the very topic that it champions—namely Win-Win.

Figure 1.3.2 : A More Optimistic Representation of Win-Win Matrix

It is my firm view that everything must be done to avoid losing.

By entering into any negotiation, when both parties are in this lower-left quadrant, a better outcome will prevail from the negotiation if neither arrives at the discussion table with the fatalistic view that both parties will lose.

1.4

THE SHORTFALLS OF THE TRADITIONAL WIN-WIN MATRIX

Key Takeaways

1. There are innumerable positive, optimistic and added-value reasons to believe in the principle of Win-Win.
2. The Win-Win Matrix has several attributes that are endearing, but it is neither positive nor optimistic.
3. Such is the disconnect between the principle of Win-Win and the Win-Win Matrix, that an alternative method is required.

WIN-WIN—THE PRINCIPLE

Win-Win is a simple concept. If donkeys can get it, there is no reason why humans cannot do so either!

Win-Win is easy to grasp. Everyone wants to win in a one-versus-another situation. Everyone understands Win-Lose. By repeating the word *win*, we understand, and can visualize, what the Win-Win concept is getting at. It is self-explanatory.

Win-Win is tangible. No matter the topic, a Win-Win outcome is quantifiable. You should be able to put a figure on what you have won.

Win-Win is positive. It is better than Lose.

Win-Win is optimistic. It helps you believe that there is a path to winning.

Win-Win is often short-term. It is a legitimate outcome that the benefits of Win-Win be felt immediately. Any Win-Win agreement is accompanied by a mutual sense of satisfaction.

Win-Win can also be long-term. For instance, in a negotiation, you might give up on something 'today', such as a lower price for a period of X months, in return for a guarantee of getting something 'tomorrow', such as a return to the original price with a Y% annual increase in future years.

Additionally, a party that is satisfied with their current relationship, partnership, or trading terms with another party is less likely to insist on sitting down and renegotiating these terms than one that is dissatisfied.

There is also a human price, in terms of workload. Any such renegotiation will inevitably be on top of the everyday business workload. At a time where businesses today are placing more and more pressure on fewer and fewer employees, time-consuming, stressful, uncomfortable, important A-Z business negotiations are unwelcome tasks.

A-Z renegotiations with important customers can also provide unwelcome business instability in a time of change. Instability is rarely good from an employee perspective.

Where there is mutual satisfaction in current trading terms between both parties, this Win-Win approach will potentially reduce the frequency of negotiations.

Win-Win is global—not in the Earth sense of the term. Although I have not done exhaustive linguistic research on the topic, I am confident the term Win-Win is understood by most cultures and people.

Win-Win is widely covered in the media. Politicians, from Donald Trump in the USA to Boris Johnson in the United Kingdom, have openly espoused their Win-Win intentions as they step to the negotiating table on complex geopolitical topics, such as, respectively, US-China relations or Brexit.

Win-Win is an elegant notion. In his book *The 7 Habits of Highly Effective People*, Stephen Covey[1] tells us 'Win-Win is a belief in the third alternative. It's not your way, nor my way. It is a better way, a higher way.'

Win-Win is a behaviour. Adversaries are far more likely to reach a Win-Win outcome if they both believe in it and, thereby, demonstrate Win-Win behaviours.

I could go on...

The notion of Win-Win has many advantages.

The Win-Win Matrix is a tool for predicting a Win-Win negotiation outcome.

WIN-WIN MATRIX

The Win-Win Matrix is a simple tool for framing Win-Win. There are many positive attributes to it.

The Win-Win Matrix is visual, like other matrixes that you might be familiar with in the business world, such as the Boston Consulting Group (BCG) Matrix for assessing potential strategies of a portfolio of products, services, or businesses.

The Win-Win Matrix, like the BCG Matrix, is something that you can simply pick up and use. There are not many business tools or models that fall into this category.

The Win-Win Matrix is simple to explain. The parameters of the Win-Win Matrix are simply explained to your team, peers, or superiors if you need to get them on board with a strategy, or situation that you have in mind.

The Win-Win Matrix is easy to understand. For the same reasons.

While this is a strength, it is also a weakness.

Like any black or white tool, its simplistic nature can lead a user to not explore alternative outcomes that might be more positive. This is particularly a risk if you find yourself positioned in one of the 'you lose' quadrants. This thereby applies to three of the four quadrants of the Win-Win Matrix. Not very Win-Win!

As far as I am concerned, this is a deal-breaker. For such an optimistic principle, how can it be that 75% of the outcomes (3 out of 4!) predict a Lose outcome.

For this to be avoided, an alternative tool is required, where your option to win cannot be so easily overlooked. Lose should not necessarily, or fatalistically, be a pre-determined outcome.

I am convinced that you can be on board with the idea of Win-Win but find yourself getting to the wrong conclusion due to the pre-conceived outcomes of the Win-Win Matrix.

We also saw in the last chapter, that the Win-Win Matrix can be not only fatalistic, but also defeatist. Particularly when it comes to the Lose-Lose quadrant.

With the exception of the few genuinely Lose-Lose scenarios that we identified in the last chapter, there is no reason why a Win-Win outcome (i.e. Win-Win but on a smaller scale!) cannot be achieved in this bottom-left quadrant of the Win-Win Matrix.

There is the human component, too. It is people that make Win-Win a reality. Win-Win is about believing. Win-Win is about listening. It is about exploring. It is about creativity. Often Win-Win invites adversaries to find a path to win where the most obvious outcome is lose. There are none of these components in the Win-Win Matrix.

An alternative tool is required to support the noble cause of Win-Win.

I suggest that the tool is Win-Win-Win.

PART 2

WIN-WIN-WIN

WIN-WIN-WIN: THE MUTUAL WIN

Key Takeaways

1. The Win-Win Matrix predicts that both sides will win in only one of the four quadrants. This does not reflect the spirit of Win-Win.
2. The new dimension to Win-Win is the Mutual Win, where specific actions allow both parties to win together.
3. Mutual Wins apply equally to external negotiations with third parties, and internal ones within your own organization.

Jimmy Carter, former president of the United States of America, famously said that 'Unless both sides win, no agreement can be permanent.'[1] This is so true. Think about it.

In your professional life, I'd like you to think about an Adversary—a customer or a supplier, a store landlord or tenant, a peer in a different function or a rival for your next promotion—with whom you have frequent discussions (let's call them negotiations), and where winning or losing is at stake.

If, in your last negotiation, you had the perception that you lost, you will probably have a sense of bitterness. You may well be smarting, or psychologically hurt, from the outcome of this discussion.

If you are a fighter, you may probably be looking for ways to provoke a rematch or bring your Adversary back to the table. If you are the opposite, you might be dreading even more the next time that you will both face each other on opposite sides of the table.

In all events, these feelings are not productive from a professional perspective. They may well take your eye off the ball on other more important business topics that require your undivided attention.

All this to say, in this scenario, whatever the outcome of your last negotiation was—your last agreement—it will not be permanent! You will seek to redress the situation.

If, on the other hand, you had both exited this same discussion with an alternative agreement, where both of you came out winning in some shape or form, there is a significantly higher chance that it will be permanent. Or at least, significantly longer-lasting, thereby allowing both parties to focus on more important business topics or priorities.

Jimmy Carter was right!

The Win-Win Matrix tells us that there is only one quadrant where both sides are equally strongly matched and both sides can Win. This is not the spirit, I believe, of Jimmy Carter's quote. Nor is it really the spirit of the principles of Win-Win. Win-Win is an optimistic approach. A constructive approach.

Surely there has to be an opportunity for both sides to Win in the other three quadrants?

In order for this to be possible, the key is to focus on the Mutual Win.

Mutually Winning is to focus on those actions or

outcomes where both sides can win together. This might sound utopian, but if you are a believer in the expression 'Where there's a will, there's a way,' then finding the Mutual Win is not only possible, it is quite plausible.

For this outcome to prevail, it is key that what you will now win, including the value of the new Mutual Win, exceeds all the potential outcomes of the other traditional Win-Win Matrix negotiations—Win-Lose, Lose-Win or Lose-Lose.

So how do you identify what a Mutual Win, or Mutual Wins, might look like?

In an external commercial negotiation, there are a certain number of relatively obvious examples:

- *Growth Bonus*: Instead of fighting on small adjustments to a price (for instance, based on current volumes), discuss more significant price changes based on volume increases. Here the key is that the agreed price changes be self-financed by the percentage growth increases in volume.
- *Agreed Stretched Objectives*: Similar to a growth bonus, a stretched objective is one where there is something on top, based on hitting an agreed stretched objective or multiple stretched objectives.
- *Year-end Rebates* (i.e. extra one-off discounts) based on specific annual targets.
- *Market-share Key Performance Indicator (KPI)–based Bonus*, in industries or markets where there are robust, recognised industry statistics. Here, certain advantages can be given to a customer on the basis of hitting an agreed market share, either in the total market, or simply in their own business. A market-share KPI Mutual Win is particularly interesting in environments where your ability to be listed, or grow your business, by other competitors is dependent on your market share within an industry or at respected competitors.

- *Distribution Increases* linked to the number of markets where a product, or service, is sold. When in a complex negotiation across multiple markets, increasing the number of markets where your products are sold could be an extremely important opportunity for a Mutual Win.
- *'You Scratch My Back, I Scratch Yours' Deals*: Here, cross-referencing targets, where advantages on product A that are in your Adversary's interest are linked to product B, which is in your interest.

Alternatively, if we were considering an internal company compensation negotiation between employers and employees, for instance, there are several Mutual Wins that could be put on the table.

- *Profit Sharing*, by having a variable component of salary to the achievement of mutually agreed profit achievement levels.
- A *Company Incentive* Scheme to motivate employees to over-achieve budgeted targets set by the company.
- For publicly listed companies, setting up a new *Stock Options* program could be a relevant example of a Mutual Win.

Other HR examples of Mutual Wins could also be:
- A *Long-Service Reward* program in organisations where staff turnover is high.
- A *No-Illness Bonus* for companies that, say, must replace blue-collar work absentees with temporary staff for each day of absence. The company could incentivize employees to not take 'inappropriate' sick leave.

These commercial and HR examples are just a few non-exhaustive ones that spring quite easily to mind and that you may well already have considered in your own business.

Once identified, each of these criteria can be quantified such that you are able to proactively establish how far you can go financially in your negotiation, based on the topic.

These are your Internal Mutual Wins, if you like.

Now let us return to, and drill down on, the External Mutual Wins, where your Adversary works in a different company. External Mutual Wins are ones where your Adversary wins too. While you might be able to identify, or guess, what their Wins might look like, the best way to identify them is most probably to simply reach out to them. Yes, simply ask them.

In asking them, you must of course be genuinely interested in listening to the answer. Your approach must be earnest and honest. My personal experience tells me that the more open, honest and interested you are, the more open, honest and intrigued your Adversary becomes. It goes without saying that, if you do not engage your Adversary, it is quite possible that you will never find out what a potential Mutual Win might be.

So there is no exhaustive list of what External Mutual Wins could potentially look like for a given Adversary. They genuinely depend on your Adversary's own business situation.

Here are just a few personal experiences that I have encountered where, without engaging my Adversary in an honest and interested way, I would never have been able to get to a Mutual Win.

Case 1: Staff Turnover Reduction

I was sitting down with an already expensive (i.e. low-profit-generating to me) customer. My company was one of their major suppliers albeit with declining annual sales. During my negotiation over the price of our products, my customer shared with me that their No. 1 issue was the (seriously) high staff turnover in their sales force. They estimated that if their staff turnover could be reduced by 20%, their total business sales could grow mechanically by 5% per year. The Mutual Win was to take the product price completely off the table and instead explore mutually beneficial investments to reducing staff turnover.

Case 2: International Door-Opening

I was facing with a particularly challenging negotiation with a domestic supplier when working for a multinational company. I could not afford the price and I had no alternative supplier to turn to. I discovered that exporting to other international subsidiaries of my company was one of their key business objectives. By focusing on what I could do to make this happen, I ensured that we took the pressure off the price negotiation that I could not afford to lose.

Case 3: Give Something Your Adversary Has Always Dreamed of But Has Never Managed to Have

As a recently appointed managing director, I had to meet my counterpart from our biggest client company. Our two companies had a historically highly confrontational relationship, despite the fact that we were both leaders in our respective business sectors. During our discussion, rather than focusing on just what was going wrong and why our business together was not at the right level, I simply asked what he dreamed of and had never got from any of his suppliers in terms of support to drive his business forward.

It turned out that this dream was something that our company could offer. We just didn't know it!

In return for making his dream come true, I allowed myself to tell him what my 'dream come true' would be with his company. Of course, I knew that this was something that he could offer. The deal was done.

The point of these examples is not to demonstrate my own personal negotiation skills, but rather to stress the importance of asking and engaging your Adversary.

Other noteworthy examples of External Mutual Wins are Intel or Lycra. They are worldwide recognized brand names and trade across multiple categories. They are key suppliers to worldwide recognized brands and negotiate to have their own brand name featured on products and/or in advertising of the brands that they supply.

Of course, there may be External Mutual Wins that your Adversary identifies that you simply cannot satisfy. This is both normal and, arguably, to be expected.

This does not mean that engaging your Adversary has been a waste of time. On the one hand, you will most probably have learnt something new about your customer and, on the other hand, you will hopefully have gained a measure of respect from your customer through the honest and earnest approach you have demonstrated towards understanding what is on their page.

In each of the three examples, there is a Mutual Win.

A Mutual Win does not mean that each party wins equally. In a Mutual Win, it may well be that one party will gain more out of it than the other. This means that it is important, where possible, to quantify what the relative Wins for each party will be such that their relative value can be taken into consideration by both parties as the negotiation plays out.

Clearly, one would hope that Party A, who has most to gain from the agreed Mutual Win, will compromise more on one or other classic Win-Lose topics, where Party B has most to lose.

Here, in their negotiation strategy, Party B should link the discussions on the Mutual Win topics to discussions on the Win-Lose topics, where they believe they have most to lose.

The Win-Win notion is somehow two-dimensional. You win, your Adversary wins. The Mutual Win adds a new, third dimension to any negotiation.

Without the Mutual Win dimension, a Win-Lose outcome is more likely in any such traditional negotiation.

It is important to emphasize that Mutual Wins do not necessarily mean the same thing to both parties.

It could be that a Mutual Win is one where both parties club together to increase their respective market shares in their respective fields of play.

Mutual Wins can be a powerful tool.

The key to understanding, and subsequently unleashing, the scale of this power is to understand your Adversary.

UNDERSTANDING YOUR ADVERSARY

Key Takeaways

1. For a Mutual Win to be accepted, it needs to be put on the table in an objective and quantified manner.
2. Starting from your understanding of your own P&L, try to gain an understanding of your Adversary's P&L in order help identify the scope and scale of potential Mutual Wins.
3. Mutual Wins can (i) be found within the P&L cost block that you are operating in, (ii) be in another cost block or (iii) be a means to grow the turnover of the company.

We all know that it takes two to tango. A negotiation is no different.

If your Adversary does not want to listen to you, your negotiation will be adversarial in every sense of the term.

This could simply be because of the temperament of your Adversary. This is not uncommon. For instance, it could be that he, or she, is adamant that they hold all the cards and will therefore seek to impose a Win-Lose on you.

It could also be that they simply have not explored the

third dimension of the Mutual Win. It may well be that they are more focused on the binary elements of Win-Lose.

In all events, you need to fully understand your Adversary in order to bring them round to:
- the items that could be on the Mutual Win table
- the quantification of these potential Mutual Wins
- together with an assessment of the ability to materialise these Mutual Wins.

We saw in the last chapter how to identify the items that can be brought to the Mutual Win table.

Now let us look at the rest of the equation.

The first place to start is a respectful attempt to understand the building blocks that make up their P&L.

First of all, let's understand in a rough-cut, generic way the principal building blocks of a business's P&L.

These building blocks are not exhaustive. I simply use them as a guide to help us illustrate how these building blocks interact and differ according to the business you are in and the business your potential Adversary is in.

To simplify matters, I have identified eight principal P&L building blocks.

Product Costs: All the costs associated with the creation of the cost of your product(s) or service(s), including packaging, shipping, raw materials, labour costs, etc.

Commercial Discounts[1]: All the reductions that a company offers on their product(s) or service(s) to ensure the sale to a customer or end consumer. These commercial discounts are expressed from the base of their published (or list) price for the product(s) or service(s)—where there is one of course—and can include various forms of price reductions, including immediate or deferred discounts, a rebate that is offered based on a time-based, or volume-based target, and so on. By their very nature, they are at the discretion of the company and therefore subject to negotiation.

Marketing Costs: All the costs that are not sales costs and that are associated with the promotion of the company's product(s) or service(s). These costs can include any advertising or sales promotions to either your customers or end consumers, displays, brochures, market research, etc. These costs in some companies include the cost of the marketing team that creates all the necessary marketing supports.

Sales Costs: All the costs of the teams associated with the commercial process of your product(s) or service(s). These sales costs could include sales store staff for a retailer, field-based sales teams (where sales are made in each customer location), headquarters-based sales teams (where sales are handled at a national/regional level to national/regional customers), customer service teams, etc.

Rent/Offices: The real-estate cost associated with the sale of your product(s) or service(s). For a retailer, this will include the costs of the stores (including rent, heating, electricity). For a company that operates regionally, this will include all costs associated with the regional network of offices.

Logistics Costs: All the costs associated with the storage, handling and delivery of your product(s) or service(s).

Admin/HQ Costs: All of the centralized costs associated with the HQ of your company, including not only the HQ office costs themselves (such as rent, heating, electricity) but also the salary costs of all the HQ functions and team members that are required to run the company and whose costs have not been accounted for in one of the other building blocks. Typically, these costs could be for the general management, finance/accounting, human resources and any other shared-services teams that a company might have.

Profit (Before Tax): What is left over after all the above business costs have been exhaustively accounted for. Hopefully, a positive number!

Now let us look at four different types of business in order to understand better the interaction between, and importance of, each of these building blocks. Here again, not only are there dozens (or hundreds…!) of different business types but also, with each type of business, there can be different weights associated with each building block.

1. **Consumer-Goods Companies** that sell products, or brands, in different wholesale channels (i.e. run by third parties) and where it is the responsibility of the company to raise awareness and demand for their products or brands. Companies selling household registered brand names such as Coca-Cola, Microsoft, Toyota, Marlboro, L'Oréal, HP, or Pampers, to name just a few, would fall into this category.

2. **Retail Companies** that sell products or services via their own distribution network. Such a network could include their own high-street, commercial-centre or factory-outlet stores or rented store space in third-party

locations such as department stores or other multi-environment stores. Retailers like Walmart, the Home Depot, Hermès, Starbucks, Zara, IKEA, Costco, Saks Fifth Avenue would be examples of companies that could fall into this category.

3. **Service-Industry Companies** that sell their services—in other words not a physical product(s)—to customers or direct to consumers. Worldwide companies such as Accenture, SAP, Netflix, YouTube, Uber, LinkedIn might fit into this category.

4. **Business-to-Business Companies** are those behind-the-scenes firms that supply the physical raw materials, parts or components that make up an end-product that is either part of a product, or part of something that is used to sell a product, to a customer or end consumer. By definition, they are behind the scenes. There are not many worldwide household-name companies that fall into this category, but Intel, Gore-Tex and Lycra are good examples that spring to mind.

There are literally millions and millions of valiant, lesser-known companies that fall into this business-to-business category.

In the below illustration, we see a bar chart representing a breakdown of how the P&L building blocks interact across these four business categories, based on a sales-revenue or gross-turnover line of 100.

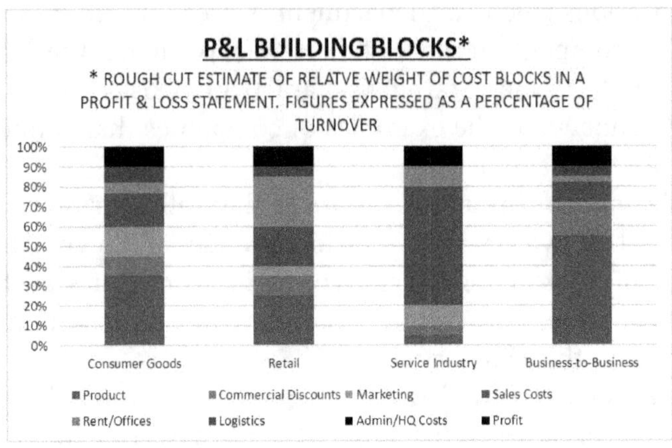

Figure 2.2.1: Profit and Loss Statement Building Blocks

For ease of comparison, let's imagine one company in each category that enjoys the same level of profitability of (say) 5% and where the admin/HQ costs are also identical when expressed as a percentage of their gross sales turnover of (say also) 5%.

Based on their turnover, we see that each business category has a P&L with a different profile, according to its business model.

For instance, a consumer-goods company will probably have the highest percentage in marketing costs and one of the lowest in terms of regional rent/offices. They invest heavily to create consumer demand in the various channels of distribution in which they operate. Invariably, as they sell through third-party retailers, they do not have a retail-store network themselves.

Retailers will have significant cost blocks in sales costs and rent/offices due to their retail network. As their stores invariably only sell their own range of products, they do not have to invest as heavily as consumer-goods companies. Their retail stores and their windows are a form of advertising in themselves.

Service-industry players are likely to have the lowest product costs but the highest sales costs, due to the (probably) inevitable human factor required to provide or sell their service.

Lastly, a busines-to-business company will probably have the biggest block in terms of product costs due to the limited added value that a company can bring to the table as a component, behind-the-scenes part of another product or service. Their marketing costs are very low. They will not have a retail store network to pay for, either.

There are three important reasons for the P&L building block exercise.

The first is to help you compare your probable inside-out understanding of your own company's P&L with this helicopter-view estimate of your Adversary's company. It will not only give you a better sensitivity as to where your Adversary is coming from, but also an improved understanding of where the relationship between your company and your Adversary's sits in the scale of their overall business.

The second will help you brainstorm potential sources of Mutual Wins:

1. **Cost-reduction ideas, within the cost block** that you operate in your Adversary's P&L. Here you should have all the information you already need.
2. **Cost-reduction ideas, in another cost block**, where, for instance, your company has expertise, clout or contacts that could be brought the table in order to mitigate Win-Lose topics within your scope.

   For example, imagine you are a supplier in the *product or marketing cost blocks*, where stock availability is an issue due to their infrequent and unpredictable bulk-order process, and they are looking for an increase in their commercial terms.

Ask yourself if there could be a Mutual Win in other cost blocks?

How about looking at the *logistics cost block* parameters of your relationship that might have a beneficial impact on your Adversary's business and benefit yours at the same time? For instance, by increasing the frequency of orders placed so as to have better real-time market visibility and a reduced number of products per order, you could perhaps reduce your stock-outs on bulk orders and allow you to increase your service levels and thereby turnover. Or, what about the *sales cost block*, which is less on the radar?

How about financing one of their sales-force incentives that otherwise they would have paid for themselves. You might be able to source 'prizes' that have a higher face value than the price you can source them. Think about:

- offering your own products, or...
- a different product that you have preferential prices on, thanks to a negotiation that has been conducted elsewhere in your company's business.

In some industries, such as bars/restaurants, biodiagnosis, hairdressing to name but a few, this practice is widespread. If we take the world of hairdressing, for instance: product manufacturers offer hairdressing furniture and accessories as a means of securing the purchase of their products at a higher price. The product manufacturers are able to negotiate significantly better prices for furniture and hairdressing accessories than an individual hairdressing salon.

Both are potential Mutual Wins that move the negotiation debate away from a Win-Lose negotiation on price or commercial discounts.

3. **Turnover-increasing ideas** designed to increase the total turnover of your Adversary's company.

For instance, let us imagine a negotiation between Company 'Alpha', a service-based retail company (such as a restaurant or hairdressing chain) and Company 'Beta', one of their principal suppliers. For Alpha's $1 million (say) turnover, the total cost to create their service is $150,000, 15% of their turnover. Beta is their biggest supplier and represents 30% of this cost, namely $45,000. Alpha believe that this is too much and are seeking to negotiate improved terms with Beta (see *Figure 2.2.2*). They are demanding an extra 10% discount.

NEGOTIATION START POINT							
Company 'Alpha' P&L - Service-based Retailer	**Today**			**Company 'Beta' Supplier to Service-based Retailer**	**Today**		
	%	**Value**			**Your % Share**	**Share Value**	
Turnover $ (Net Sales after all discounts etc)	100.0%	1,000,000					
Cost of Goods (% of turnover $)	15.0%	150,000		Your Products (as a share of their Total Cost of Goods)	30%	45,000	
Marketing (Advertising & Promotion)	10.0%	100,000					
Sales Costs (Fixed & Variable)	45.0%	450,000					
Overhead, Costs (rent, HQ/Admin/IT costs, etc, …)	20.0%	200,000					
Profit $	10.0%	100,000					

Figure 2.2.2: Negotiation Start Point

In this Win-Lose scenario, if Beta accepts Alpha's demand, what Beta loses, Alpha wins (see *Figure 2.2.3*). An extra 10% discount represents $4,500 in lost revenue (and potentially profit) for Beta for the same volume. For Alpha, this reduction falls directly to the bottom line. Beta may simply refuse to accept Alpha's demands.

WIN, WIN, WIN!

WIN-LOSE SCENARIO						
Company 'Alpha' P&L - Service-based Retailer	WIN		Company 'Beta' Supplier to Service-based Retailer	LOSE		
	%	Value			Your % Share	Share Value
Turnover $ (Net Sales after all discounts etc)	100.0%	1,000,000				
Cost of Goods (% of turnover $)	14.6%	145,500	Adversary Demand for 10% Increase in discounts	28%	40,500	
Marketing (Advertising & Promotion)	10.0%	100,000				
Sales Costs (Fixed & Variable)	45.0%	450,000				
Overhead, Costs (rent, HQ/Admin/IT costs, etc, …)	20.0%	200,000				
Profit $	10.5%	104,500				
Impact on Alpha's Profitability		4,500	Impact on Beta's Profitability		- 4,500	

Figure 2.2.3: Win-Lose Negotiation Scenario

An alternative Win-Win plan, based on increasing Alpha's turnover, can be identified.

Instead of giving an extra discount, Beta could accept that they'd invest (say) $500 in targeted activities, for instance, to drive an increase in Alpha's turnover by (say) an additional $20.000, a growth of 2% in their turnover.

An alternative Win-Win plan, based on increasing Alpha's turnover, can be identified.

An extra 2% in their turnover will generate an extra $20,000. Their cost of goods will increase by 2% ($3,000) in line with the turnover, but the $17,000 is pure profit! This is a significantly better outcome for Alpha than the $4,500 that was originally on the table (see *Figure 2.2.4*). In fact, Alpha will be better off financially in the Win-Win scenario, even if a mere 0.6% increase in turnover is achieved ($6,000 in turnover, $900 increase in costs and thereby $5,100 increase in profitability).

WIN-WIN NEGOTIATION SCENARIO						
Company 'Alpha' P&L - Service-based Retailer	WIN		Company 'Beta' Supplier to Service-based Retailer	WIN		
	%	Value		Your % Share	Share Value	
Turnover $ (Net Sales after all discounts etc)	100.0%	1,020,000				
Cost of Goods (% of turnover $)	15%	153,000	No Increase in discounts	30%	45,900	
Marketing (Advertising & Promotion)	10.0%	100,000	Investment in Activities to Grow Turnover by 2%		- 500	
Sales Costs (Fixed & Variable)	45.0%	450,000				
Overhead, Costs (rent, HQ/Admin/IT costs, etc, …)	20.0%	200,000				
Profit $	10.0%	117,000				
Impact on Alpha's Profitability		17,000	Impact on Beta's Profitability		400	

Figure 2.2.4: Win–Win Scenario

If Alpha accepts this proposal, we see that Beta sees their profitability grow by $400, instead of declining by $4.500.

With this perfect Win-Win outcome, Alpha will be $17.000 more profitable; Beta $400. These outcomes are far better for both players than the $4,500 Win-Lose stakes at the outset.

Seen this way, it's clear that this Mutual Win approach has opened up a massive area for negotiation on the level of investment that Beta might want to make in order to support the 2% turnover increase.

To secure the deal confidently, Beta could offer more than $5,000 investment and still be in a better P&L

position than the opening Win-Lose scenario.

Beta might also feel confident that if they put $5,000 on the table, Alpha's turnover might increase by over 2%! The vicious circle on price reduction has now turned into a virtuous circle on turnover growth.

There are two key takeaways from such a Mutual Win scenario.

1. Both parties can be better off. They both benefit from the turnover generated by the extra volume, albeit they benefit differently and not necessary equally. Their interests are aligned.
2. The negotiation can completely move away from a binary Win-Lose discussion on price to an added-value discussion on growth. Seriously powerful!

It is therefore in both Alpha's and Beta's interests to pursue this Win-Win line of negotiation based on an increase in Alpha's turnover.

Utopian, perhaps. Worth a shot, definitely!

This brings us to the third reason why this exercise is so useful. Namely, where does your Adversary sit in their organization? What is his/her responsibility? What is his/her performance judged on by his/her company?

If, looking at the above example, your Adversary is not judged at all on company turnover or profitability, then this Mutual Win is unlikely to fly.

To make it fly, you will need to get your boss, or your boss's boss involved, such that the negotiation takes place at the level where your proposed Mutual Win can be a relevant, serious topic.

Do not be afraid to do this from an internal perspective! By integrating these senior stakeholders, I guarantee that you will score points with your hierarchy for thinking outside the box and working creatively in your company's interest, even if the negotiation of the Mutual Win ultimately does not play out the way you anticipated.

Once they are on board, and in order not to upset your Adversary, it is vital that this right-level person—your boss, your boss's boss, or suchlike—reach out to their counterpart in the Adversary's organisation to frame the discussions between your two companies. It can be done face to face, by telephone or by email.

This does not mean that this right-level person has to handle the details of the negotiation. Far from it!

Once the new scope, including that of your planned Mutual Win, has been agreed by these two stakeholders, you will have the liberty to discuss all subject matters that are in this new scope. From now on, you should simply keep him/her updated on progress.

Alternatively, you may well want to have the support of your hierarchy during the negotiation phases. In this case, you might welcome the intervention of your hierarchy to validate the outcomes as they play out.

All that to say, when it comes to identifying, quantifying and negotiating Mutual Win ideas, understanding your Adversary is a *must*.

In my experience, the curiosity and ingenuity with which you consider all aspects of your business relationship with your Adversary will also be appreciated by them.

When this process of understanding your Adversary's P&L is conducted systematically, you will also discover that your understanding of your Adversary's business will improve exponentially.

Over time, this ever-more-accurate understanding will only be a benefit to you. Going forward, it will, quite probably, allow you to predict more proactively trends, future problems and solutions, and potentially new opportunities that are important in your collaboration. Minter Dial and Caleb Storkey[2] go one step further in their book *Futureproof: How to Get Your Business Ready for the Next Disruption*—'By putting ourselves in our customers' shoes, we can create validated, meaningful and lasting experiences.'

There you go... another Mutual Win!

THE WIN-WIN-WIN PYRAMID: A NEW MODEL

Key Takeaways

1. The Win-Win-Win Pyramid is a new model that adds the extra dimension of the Mutual Win—the Win that is in both parties' interests.
2. The Win-Win-Win Pyramid offers a more optimistic approach to preparing for any potential Win-Win negotiation.
3. By adjusting the Equilibrium Point of the Win-Win-Win Pyramid, we can visualize the potential outcome(s) of any given negotiation.

To bring in this third dimension of the Mutual Win, a new visualization tool is required. The traditional Win-Win Matrix (see *Figure 2.3.1*) has not only the shortcomings that we looked at in Part 1, but also it neither captures, nor ensures that the spotlight is correctly put on, the potential scope for Mutual Wins.

In this new model, there is a third axis to identify what is in the interest of both parties—the Mutual Win. This axis complements the other two axes that stake out the individual interests of each of the two parties—you and your Adversary.

The new model needs also to reflect the dynamic nature of any negotiation, where:
- We capture the relative strength, or weakness, of both parties—one of the positive elements of the traditional Win-Win Matrix.
- We also understand where each party potentially stands.
- We thereby get a prediction of how balanced, or un-balanced, the negotiation is going to be.

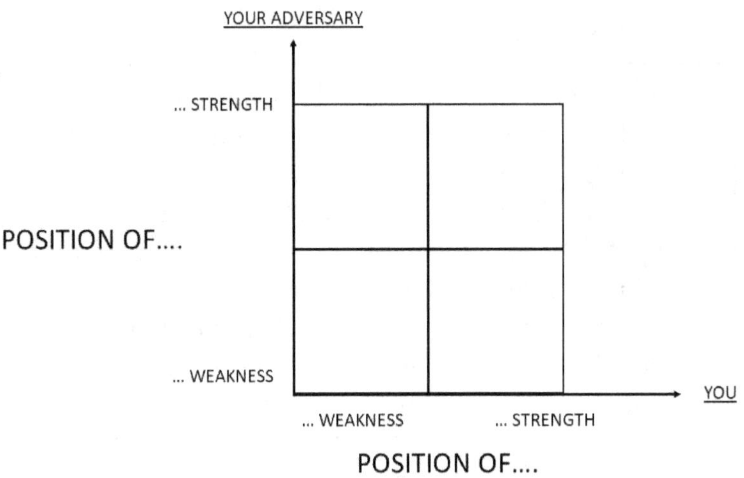

Figure 2.3.1: Win-Win Matrix Traditional Model

This notion of 'balance' is an important component in helping each party, particularly the one in the weakest position, prepare for the negotiation and get the best possible outcome.

When these parameters are all combined, this gives us the Win-Win-Win Pyramid.

First of all, let's look at the shape of the object. You could call it a triangle. I see it as a pyramid that is viewed from above (see *Figure 2.3.2*).

What I like about the image of the Pyramid is that it gives one a sense of scale and thus a better sense of the material, most probably financial, stakes that are in the balance in any important business negotiation. This sense of scale is important to always keep in sight as sometimes the very livelihood, or financial viability, of a company can be at stake in serious make-or-break negotiations.

With the Win-Win-Win Pyramid, we see that there are three axes that capture outcomes or topics:

1. Only in *your* interests
2. Only in *your Adversary's* interests
3. In *both* your interests, thereby capturing the scope for Mutual Wins.

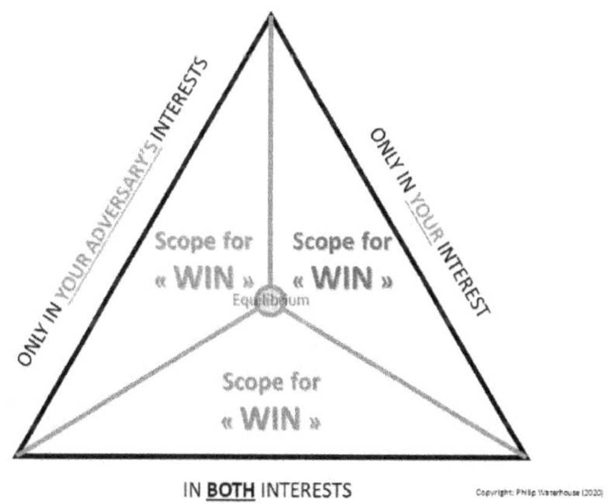

Figure 2.3.2: Win-Win-Win Pyramid

In the middle, or apex, of the Pyramid, we see the circle, the Equilibrium Point. The position of this Equilibrium Point can move:

• From the *left* (i.e. away from your Adversary, towards you) to the *right* (i.e. away from you, towards your

Adversary) in order to gauge the relative *strength*, or *weakness*, of both parties as we saw in the traditional Win-Win Matrix.

• *Up* or *down*, according to the scope of the potential Mutual Wins that you have identified.

I am sure you can picture that as the Equilibrium Point moves, so too does the shape and mass of the Pyramid.

It becomes lopsided, which also gives an immediate visual understanding of whether the negotiation is likely to be *balanced* or *unbalanced*, just as we saw in the Win-Win Matrix.

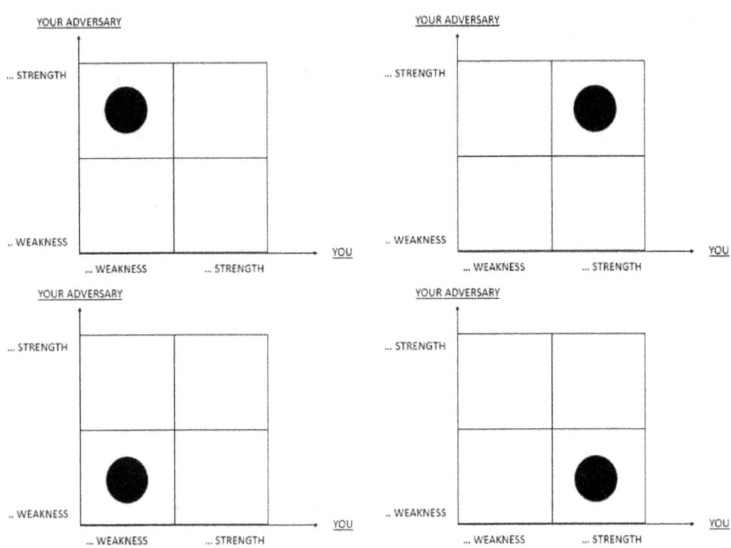

Figure 2.3.3: Traditional Win-Win Matrix - Step 1: Identify Your Position

Before we dive into how we use the Win-Win-Win Pyramid, let's quickly remind ourselves of the four positions, or quadrants, of the traditional Win-Win Matrix (see *Figure 2.3.3*) and the two steps required to get to the predicted outcome.

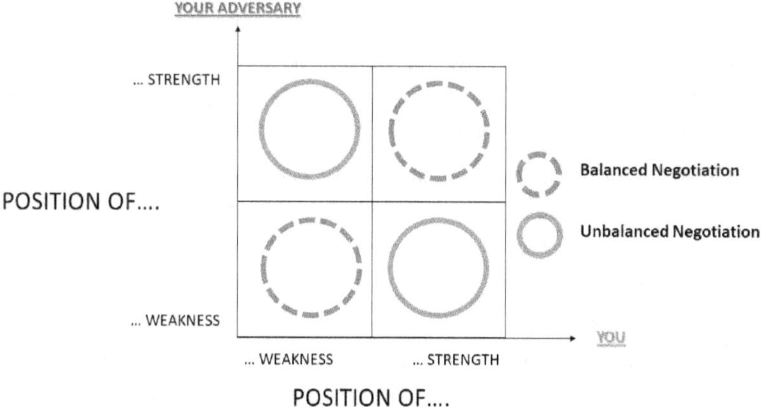

Figure 2.3.4 : Win-Win Matrix - Is the Negotiation Balanced or Unbalanced?

Step 1: Identify Your Position

The matrix is split into four quadrants. If the relative positions to one another are similar (see *Figure 2.3.4*), the negotiation is set in a *balanced* position. If one player is in a stronger position than the other, then the situation is clearly *unbalanced*.

With the Win-Win-Win Pyramid, the first step is identical (see *Figure 2.3.5*).

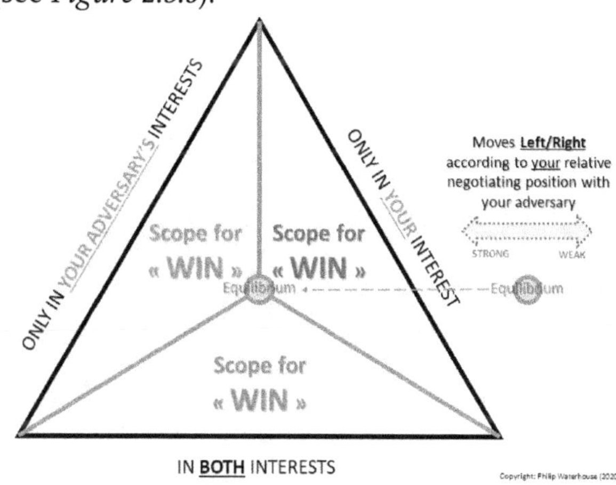

Figure 2.3.5: Win-Win-Win Pyramid Positions - Step 1: Identify Your Position

Start with the perfect Equilibrium Point (i.e. right in the middle of the Pyramid). If your Adversary is in a stronger position, we move the Equilibrium horizontally accordingly to the right. Your Adversary is in a stronger position as their scope for winning is greater than yours.

As the Equilibrium Point is then moved to the right, we see the face of your Adversary's pyramid that captures the scope for Win increases. At the same time, your own face that captures the scope for Win gets smaller.

Visually, not only can we see the stakes of the negotiation, but we can also almost physically feel the weaker party being squeezed into a smaller, more uncomfortable space.

This alone is a good reminder to the party with the weaker hand.

This exercise yields three potential different Pyramids.

In Position A, we see that both parties are well-matched. The balance of power is neither in your, nor your Adversary's, hands. The negotiation, no matter whether you are both equally weak or equally strong, is sitting in a *balanced* position.

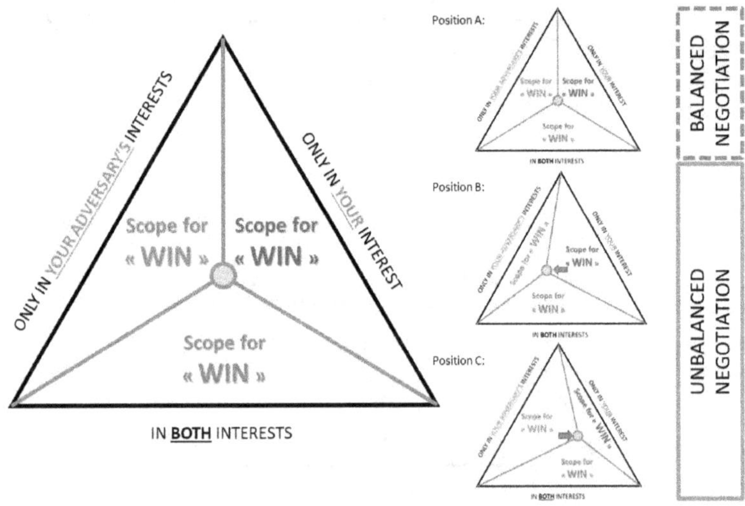

Figure 2.3.6: Win-Win-Win Pyramid - Step 1: Outcomes

In Position B, the Equilibrium Point has moved to the left, as depicted by the arrow. Here we clearly see that you potentially have the upper hand and your Adversary is squeezed into a smaller space. In simple terms, based on the you/your Adversary dimension, you are in the winning zone. Your Adversary is in the losing zone.

In Position C, however, the Equilibrium Point has moved to the right, as shown by the arrow. The tables have turned! You are the one that is squeezed. Your Adversary is in a stronger position. Based on the you/your Adversary dimension, we are looking at Lose-Win.

In both Position B and Position C, the negotiation start point is *unbalanced*.

Step 2: Identify the Scope for Mutual Wins

In Step 2, we move the Equilibrium Point vertically from where it ended up in Step 1. If there is plenty of meat-on-the-bone potential for Mutual Wins, we move the Equilibrium up.

If, after an exhaustive process (as we saw in the previous Chapter 2.2), there is little scope for Mutual Wins, then the Equilibrium should be moved down.

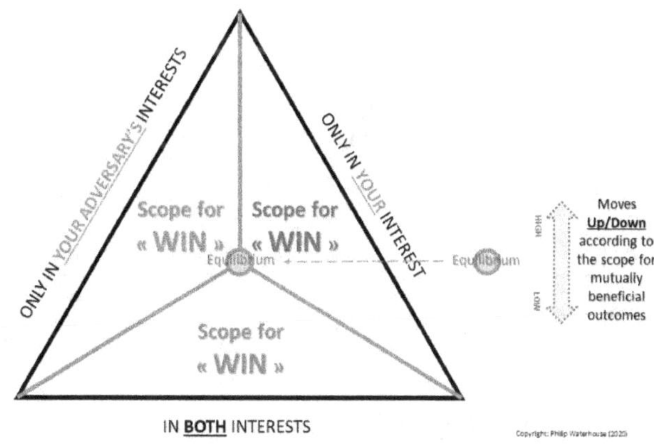

Figure 2.3.7: Win-Win-Win Pyramid
- Step 2: Identify the Scope for Mutual Wins

This exercise delivers the definitive position of the Equilibrium, dependent on the outcome of Step 1.

The significance of this final Equilibrium Point gives us an appreciation of what each party potentially has to play with.

Your situation is that:
- You have the sum of your own *scope for Win* plus the *scope for Win* that is mutually in both interests. Equally, your Adversary has the sum of their own *scope for Win* face, plus the *scope for Win* that is in both interests.
- You should quantify the full scale of the Mutual Wins to minimize your Adversary's potential to impose on them the topics that are only in their interests (and thereby not in your interests). At the same time, you maximize your own potential Wins.

Let's look at the outcomes individually.

First, the balanced negotiation position we saw earlier in Position 1.

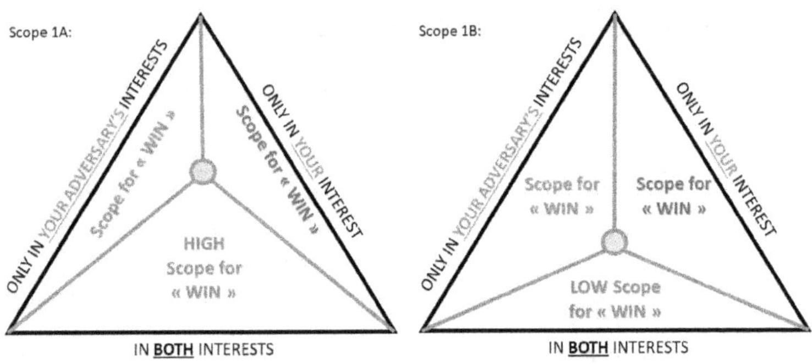

Figure 2.3.8: Win-Win-Win Pyramid - Balanced Mutual Wins

Here (see *Figure 2.3.8*), if there is high scope for Mutual Wins that are in both parties' interests, then we will end up with Scope 1A.

If there is little scope, then the scenario will be Scope 1B. Now let's look at the Equilibrium Points, where we saw an unbalanced situation coming out of Step 1 (see Figure 2.3.9).

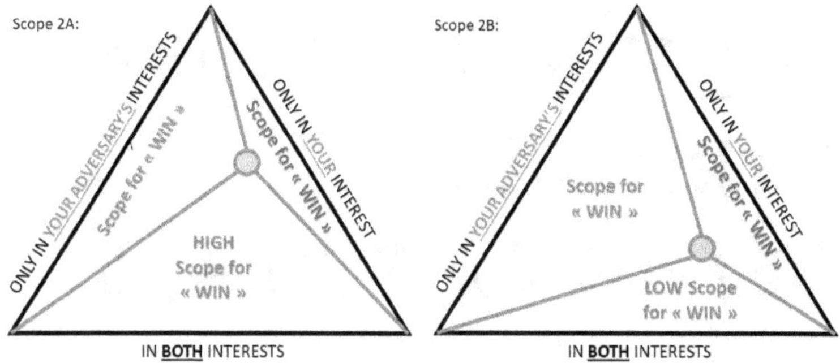

Figure 2.3.9: Win-Win-Win Pyramid - Unbalanced Mutual Wins 1

Here, we see the scenario where the deck is not stacked in your favour. If there is high scope for Mutual Wins, we end up with Scope 2A above. If you have identified only limited Mutual Wins, then we end up with Scope 2B above.

Finally, when the decks appear to be stacked in your favour (see *Figure 2.3.10*), we see Scope 3A if there is a lot of Mutual Win potential, and Scope 3B if there is not.

With Steps 1 and 2 behind us, we can now look at the potential outcomes and work on our strategy to maximize the outcome of the negotiation.

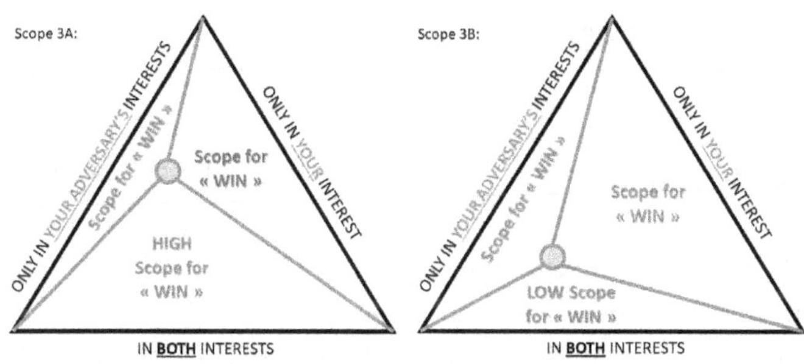

Figure 2.3.10: Win-Win-Win Pyramid - Unbalanced Mutual Wins 2

2.4

THE WIN-WIN-WIN PYRAMID: BETTER OUTCOMES

Key Takeaways

1. Whereas there are only four outcome quadrants in the Win-Win Matrix, the Win-Win-Win Pyramid has eight.
2. Given the dynamic nature of the Equilibrium Point, every Win-Win-Win Pyramid is potentially different.
3. The potential outcomes of the Win-Win-Win Pyramid are more optimistic than with the Win-Win Matrix. Each stakeholder's position is the sum of what is exclusively in their interests and those in their mutual interests.

In the last chapter, we were introduced to the Win-Win-Win Pyramid, with:

- its extra dimension—the Mutual Wins that are potentially in the interests of both parties,
- and the dynamic placement of the Equilibrium Point, which allows us to visualize the stakes that are at hand.

In this chapter we will look at the outcomes and compare them to the outcomes of the traditional Win-Win Matrix.

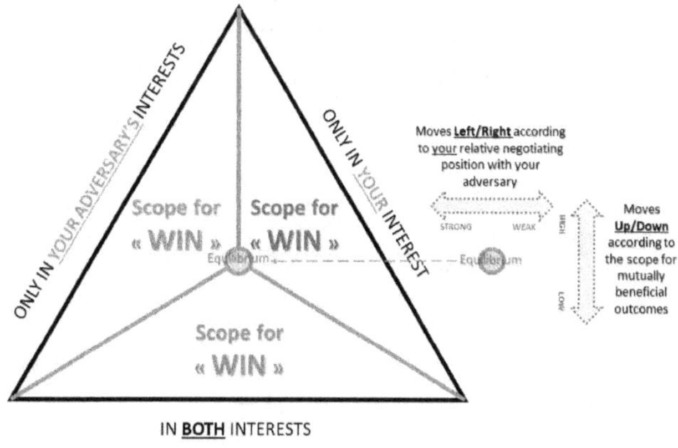

Figure 2.4.1: Win-Win-Win Pyramid

TRADITIONAL WIN-WIN MATRIX OUTCOMES

Let's start by reminding ourselves of these four outcomes.

#1 Balanced Negotiation: Both Sides Have Winning Hands
WIN-WIN, the top-right quadrant.

#2 Unbalanced Negotiation: You Are in a Stronger Position
WIN-LOSE, the bottom-right quadrant.

#3 Unbalanced Negotiation: You Are in a Weaker Position
LOSE-WIN, the top-left quadrant.

#4 Balanced Negotiation: Neither of You Is in a Strong Position
LOSE-LOSE, the bottom-left quadrant.

Now let's drill down on the outcomes of the Win-Win-Win Pyramid.

In doing so, I would like you, the reader, to think of a Win-Win negotiation that you have either already conducted yourself, or heard about, or one that you can imagine in your head.

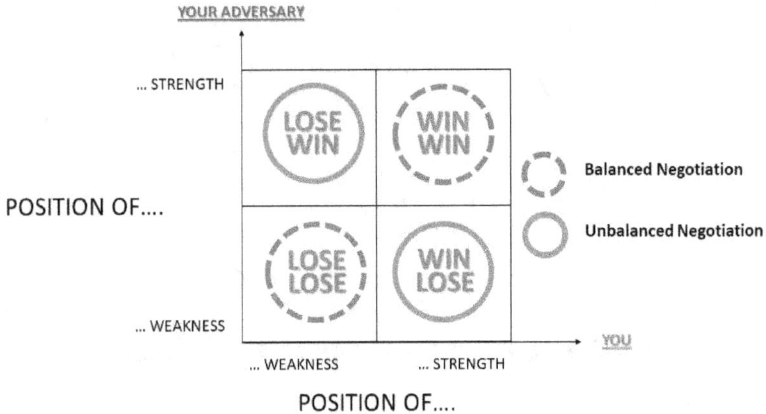

Figure 2.4.2: Win-Win Matrix Outcomes

The question we must ask ourselves as we run through these scenarios is whether, objectively, by using the Win-Win-Win Pyramid, there is or could have been an alternative, better outcome to the negotiation.

WIN-WIN-WIN PYRAMID OUTCOMES VS. TRADITIONAL WIN-WIN MATRIX

At face value, we will see that there are eight outcomes or scenarios. In reality, within each of the eight outcomes, there are infinite variations, depending on the precise position of the Equilibrium Point. A bit more to the left for one, a bit higher for the other.

No Win-Win-Win Pyramid will be the same.

For instance, let us imagine you are in a sales role where you have to embark on what appears to be the same timely (say: annual) negotiation with 10 customers who operate in the same commercial space. I would expect that each of your Adversary's companies will have different DNAs. Your power in their businesses will not be identical. It may well be that your product mix is not the same. It is quite probable that the potential Mutual Wins will not be the same, either. Accordingly, there will be 10 different Equilibrium Points—one for each company.

Given this, each negotiation needs to be prepared differently and each negotiation plan of attack defined according to its merits.

Each Win-Win-Win Pyramid will literally look different.

Plot each of these 10 different Win-Win-Win Pyramids next to each other before you embark on the process of this negotiation tour, and you will also be able to visualise the negotiation landscape that you face. Trust me, you will get an immediate visual sense of the process that you are about to embark on, together with an immediate picture of where the opportunities and threats are.

For now, though, let's look at these eight outcomes by comparing them to the quadrants of the traditional Win-Win Matrix.

#1 Balanced Negotiation: Both Sides Have Winning Hands

The parties here are equally matched. The opportunity is on the table for both parties to win in this scenario.

The Win-Win Matrix predicts a Win-Win outcome. There is no reason for this scenario not to play out, if both parties play their parts in good faith.

The Win-Win-Win Pyramid is also positive (see *Figure 2.4.3*). In Outcome 1A, we see that there are a number of potential Mutual Wins; in Outcome 1B, there are fewer.

When comparing the Win-Win-Win Pyramid outcomes with that of the Win-Win Matrix, the question is whether the two negotiating parties will negotiate a more mutually beneficial deal if the Mutual Wins are given a spotlight, as in the Win-Win-Win Pyramid, than with the Win-Win Matrix where Mutual Wins are not.

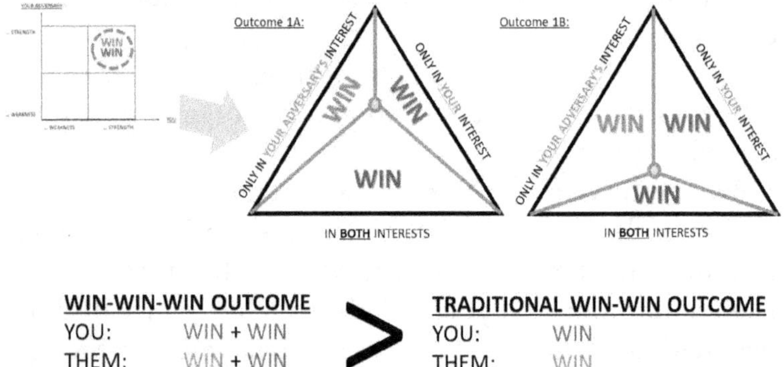

Figure 2.4.3: Win-Win-Win Pyramid
Comparing the Outcomes: Outcomes 1A & 1B

Objectively, the spotlight can only help the quality of the outcome. It cannot hinder it.

Additionally, I am convinced that when two parties agree to implement a project that has been identified by both as in their mutual interest, the partnership between the two parties will be stronger. When it comes to the necessary follow-up of the implementation of this project, their language will be identical. Their desire for the right results for the project will be aligned.

#2 Unbalanced Negotiation: You Are in a Stronger Position

The parties are not equally matched (see *Figure 2.4.4*). Based on the analysis of your respective situations, you have the upper hand. Your Adversary does not.

Clearly, the temptation here is for you to use your stronger position to ensure that you absolutely get the outcome that you are looking for. After all, you can call the shots. This is your prerogative.

Interestingly in this scenario, the outcome appears binary. You will win. Your Adversary will have no choice but to accept your demands.

A traditional Win-Win Matrix predicts therefore Win-Lose.

Without wanting to have your cake and eat it, the task you have in front of you is to consider the opportunities for Mutual Wins nonetheless—as shown in Outcome 2A if they are numerous, and in Outcome 2B if they are not.

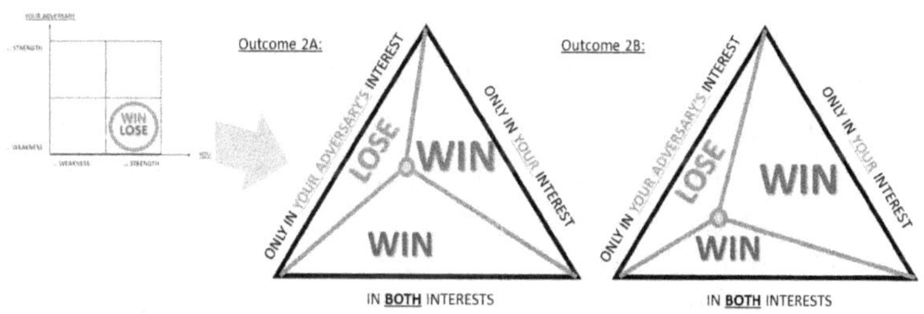

Figure 2.4.4: Win-Win-Win Pyramid
Comparing the Outcomes: Outcomes 2A & 2B

This will establish:

1. Whether there is an even better outcome for you if these Mutual Wins are fully explored.
2. Whether you are prepared to make any concessions to your You Win/Your Adversary Loses hand. This is a key point, as the implementation of the Mutual Win may well mean that your Adversary has to make certain investments at the outset, as we saw in Chapter 2.1, in order to reap the mutual benefits.

As you hold the cards, it is quite probable that the call will be yours as to whether the Mutual Win can/will be implemented.

Here are a few pointers that I suggest you should take into consideration to help you make this call:

- *Long-Term vs Short-Term*: You may recall the quote from Jimmy Carter that we saw in Chapter 2.1: 'Unless both sides win, no deal can be permanent.' It is human nature that if you lose, there will be resentment towards the winner. The same is true in a financial context. I put it to you that you will get more out of your Adversary in the long term if you ask a little less than you might be able to impose on the binary Win-Lose topics, and a little more on the Mutual Win topics; there will ultimately be a better Win-Win-Win Pyramid outcome than the traditional Win-Win Matrix one.

- *Next Time Round*: There are some negotiations where the balance of power can move from you to your Adversary and then from your Adversary to you. We see this daily in a sporting context. This can also be the case in internal negotiations—for instance, between employer and employee, two different teams or functions or between you and your boss. In these circumstances, it can be wise not to impose too significant a loss on your opponent, because you never know when the situations will be reversed. It is often a good idea to bear in mind the expression 'Every dog has his day.' I do.

- *Keeping Them Onboard*: In any relationship, it is important to keep your Adversary onboard. We looked at the long-term vs. short-term and next-time-round considerations a moment ago, but in business, there are also the unexpected events that come up. Unexpected events can be both positive—a new opportunity that your business would like to pursue and that needs support from potential adversaries for it to happen— or negative—a new challenge that needs some form of support from potential adversaries to make it happen. While these instances are, by definition, unexpected, and therefore difficult to predict, you will know whether you operate in a business environment where unexpected events are more or less likely to happen. If you are judged by your company on the ability to handle these unexpected events, or whether unexpected events can have a material impact on your results, you might want to ensure that your Adversary has something left in the bank to support these unexpected events.

#3 Unbalanced Negotiation: You Are in a Weaker Position

There is no more unpleasant situation to be faced with than this one.

You are in a weaker position than your Adversary. At first glance, you are staring at a You Lose/Your Adversary Wins situation (see *Figure 2.4.5*).

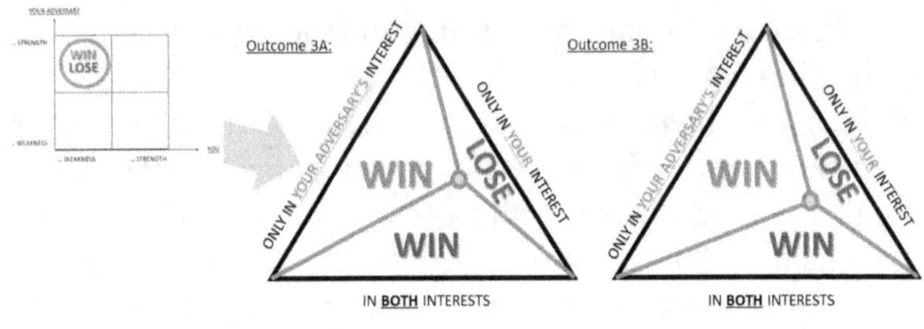

*Figure 2.4.5: Win-Win-Win Pyramid
Comparing the Outcomes: Outcomes 3A & 3B*

To be perfectly honest, when you are in this scenario the exhaustive analysis of Mutual Wins is your best call to action—see Outcome 3A if there are significant Mutual Wins and 3B if there are not.

The better you understand the cost/benefit of each Mutual Win, the better potential you have of minimizing your losing hand.

In this scenario, there is a clear distinction between Outcomes 3A and 3B. Specifically,

- *Significant Mutual Win Opportunities* (Outcome 3A): Where there are many opportunities—either in number or in financial terms—then already your hand looks stronger. Indeed, there can be a stage where, given the scale of the Mutual Wins or given your unique position to make a Mutual Win happen, this can transform the balance in your negotiation such that the odds are no longer stacked against you.

- *Insignificant Mutual Win Opportunities* (Outcome 3B): All potential Mutual Wins make your hand better than it was before. Better than it was without them. Each Mutual

Win needs to be closely analysed from both your and your Adversary's perspectives. You need to understand what commitments, financial and human, you might have to make to put the topic(s) on the agenda in order to take off, or at least take the heat off, the more classic Win-Lose ones that you are facing—for instance, classic demands for increased discounts/lower prices.

In this scenario, the ball is in your court to spark the interest in exploring all the advantages of the Mutual Wins. It is your job to bring your Adversary to the Mutual Win table.

In doing so, it is also your role to look at the direct Win-Lose topics—the ones where you are on the losing side, that you want to take off the table or water down.

In summary, your Win-Win-Win outcomes will be better than the traditional Win-Win Matrix ones depending on your ability to blend the direct Win-Lose topics together with the Mutual Wins that you bring to the table.

In all scenarios, the potential for a better outcome is there. The more you know your Adversary, the better your chance of realising this potential.

#4 Balanced Negotiation: Neither of You Is in a Strong Position

The Win-Win Matrix predicts a Lose-Lose outcome. I contest this predicted outcome.

Unless you are in one of the exceptional situations that we explored in Part 1, there is no reason for a better scenario not to play out, particularly if both parties play their parts in good faith. While neither of you is in a strong position, the power is balanced. Nobody has the upper hand. Nobody can impose on the other.

I would frankly rather take this negotiation scenario than the one we looked at last. I am convinced that, given the same hand, any party can come out of a negotiation with a better outcome against an equally weak Adversary than if the Adversary was in a stronger position.

While being in this scenario might appear to be the worst, most miserable, quadrant to be in for the traditional Win-Win Matrix, it is not the case with the Win-Win-Win Pyramid.

The Win-Win-Win Pyramid takes this on board. As we see in the potential outcomes (see *Figure 2.4.6*), there is no fatalistic expectation of loss. Neither party may be in a position to win big, but there is no reason why both cannot win something out of the situation, even if it is on a smaller scale.

So, visually speaking, instead of 'WIN', we should shoot for 'win'.

Indeed, as we see below, to get a better Win-Win-Win Pyramid outcome than the traditional Win-Win Matrix one, the challenge is to work to a plan where:

<u>Win-Win-Win Pyramid</u>		<u>Win-Win Matrix</u>
WIN + Mutual Win	>	**Lose**

I am sure we have all faced more difficult business challenges in our professional lives. This challenge should not be underestimated, however.

Once again, there are two outcomes (see *Figure 2.4.6*).

Where there are significant Mutual Win opportunities, we are looking at Outcome 4A. If there are few, then we are looking at Outcome 4B.

Unlike in the last scenario, as the negotiation is balanced, each party has an equal right to put the Mutual Wins on the table.

What is key in this scenario is that unlike in the last unbalanced one, the advantages of each Mutual Win need to be fully explored prior to the negotiation. Here is why.

In a traditional Win-Lose discussion, such as discount or price discussions (say), what one party wins, the other loses commensurately.

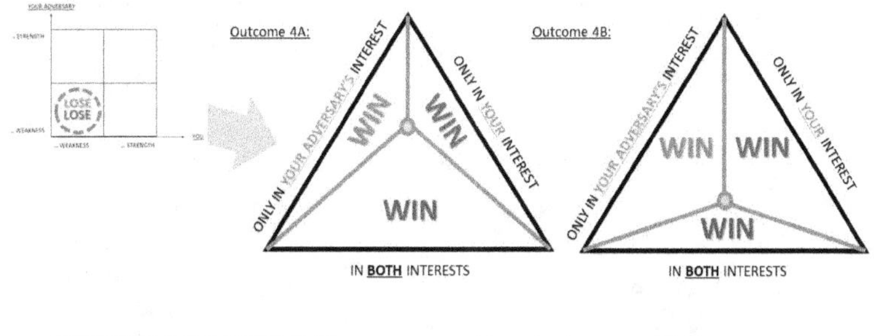

Figure 2.4.6: Win-Win-Win Pyramid
Comparing the Outcomes: Outcomes 4A & 4B

With a Mutual Win, the relationship will most probably be different. While it might be in both of your interests, both parties will win but in different measures. Calculate them. This must be taken into consideration when the Mutual Win topics are put on the table.

CONCLUSION

It's not a done deal, but there is every reason to expect that when using this new model, the Win-Win-Win Pyramid has a good chance of helping you to a better outcome than the traditional Win-Win Matrix.

In the Win-Win Matrix, there are four simple (simplistic?) outcomes. With the Win-Win-Win Pyramid, there are eight different scenarios (see *Figure 2.4.7*).

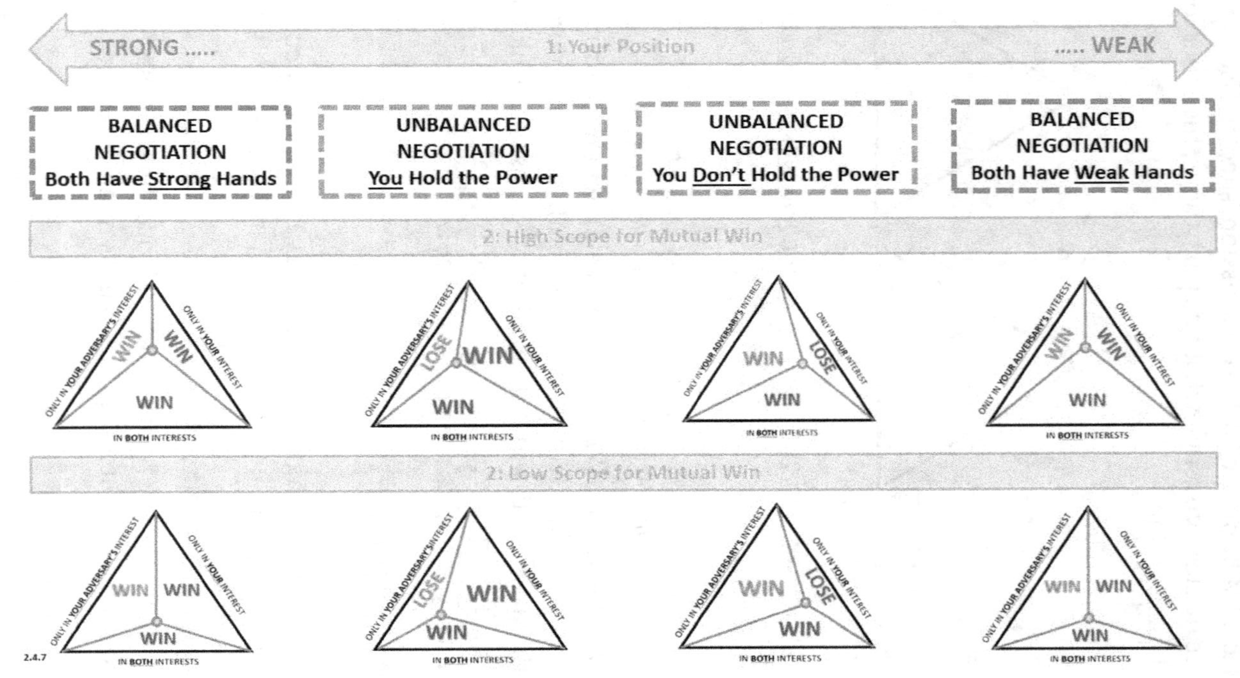

Figure 2.4.7: Win-Win-Win Pyramid Outcomes Summary

Each scenario has innumerable nuances that depend on your understanding of the Equilibrium Point's location.

More optimistically, with the Win-Win-Win Pyramid there is no place for a fatalistic Lose-Lose outcome. This does not mean that this potential outcome does not exist.

Using the Win-Win-Win Pyramid, you can only end up in the Lose-Lose space once all other avenues, including Mutual Wins, have been explored.

The personalised appreciation of the scope for Mutual Wins will also dictate how you prepare for the negotiation. The greater the scope, the stronger your position.

So, no matter the outcome relative to the Win-Win Matrix, the Win-Win-Win Pyramid is more personalized. It is tailored to your Adversary's DNA. As each customer has a different DNA, the scope and scale for Mutual Wins will be different, leading to a different Equilibrium Point.

In other words, if the traditional Win-Win Matrix is the game Noughts and Crosses (or Tic-Tac-Toe in the U.S.), then the Win-Win-Win Pyramid is Connect 4 (by Hasbro). In both cases, the objective is to create a line, but by adding the extra vertical dimension, the game is more visual and has multiple new outcomes.

If you are a visual person, like me, the Win-Win-Win Pyramid will also give you an instant 3D appreciation of the stakes.

The best example of this is Outcome 3A, which we looked at earlier (see *Figure 2.4.8*)—an unbalanced negotiation where you are holding the losing hand.

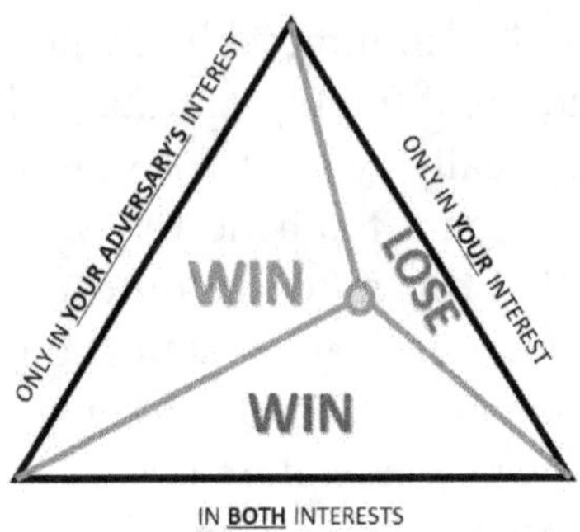

Figure 2.4.8: Win-Win-Win Pyramid Outcome 3A

On the face of it, the odds are stacked against you. You are squeezed into a smaller space relative to your Adversary. It is understandable that you are not necessarily looking forward to your negotiation. But thanks to the scale of the Mutual Wins, which we see in the bottom face of the Pyramid, the probably dark prospect of your negotiation should seem somehow brighter.

Your challenge here is to bring the focus of your negotiation onto the Mutual Wins and thereby minimize the consequences of the binary Win-Lose topics where you hold the losing hand.

Good luck!

2.5

WHAT IF YOUR ADVERSARY DOES NOT BELIEVE IN WIN-WIN?

Key Takeaways

1. If you do not know whether your Adversary believes in Win-Win, you must find out.
2. Completing the Win-Win-Win Pyramid will help you identify (i) who holds the balance of power, (ii) what the potential Mutual Wins might look like and (iii) what is the right level to find out the answer.
3. The Yes Staircase is a useful tool to help convince even the most challenging Adversary to accept the notion of Win-Win.

It cannot be taken as a given that your Adversary is on the same page as you. They might not believe in the notion of Win-Win. They might not be familiar with it.

I am not talking about the Win-Win Matrix, per se. I am referring more to the principle of Win-Win: the fact that two parties can find a mutually satisfactory outcome in which they both believe that they've achieved a positive outcome. That they have won!

To get the answer to the question 'Are you on board with the notion of Win-Win?' you are going to have to find out!

You may already know your Adversary well enough to have the answer.

If they are *on board*, fast forward.

If you know that they are *not on board*, then read on. All is not lost!

This chapter aims to:

1. Help you not only get the answer to this key question, but also
2. Ensure that, even if they are not on the Win-Win page today, they will be by the time you sit down to do the serious talking.

The first key point is that you need to embrace the topic proactively.

The starting point is to have taken a first stab at completing the Win-Win-Win Pyramid.

For three simple reasons.

1. Who Holds the Balance of Power?

You need to understand how balanced the negotiation will be.

If *you hold the power*, then you can potentially impose your point of view. For instance, you can inform you Adversary either:

1. At the outset of your negotiation, that you are a firm believer in Win-Win and that you would like to explore Win-Win opportunities as you enter in the discussion, or
2. During the negotiation, once you sense that discussions on the Win-Lose topics are getting challenging.

This is your call.

If *you do not hold the better hand*, then you need to choose the right moment to table the subject. To help you decide the right moment, let us move to reason #2.

2. What Are the Mutual Wins?

Next, you must explore the Mutual Wins, answering the following questions:
1. What are the Mutual Wins?
2. What is the financial potential of each of these Mutual Wins?
3. In which P&L cost block are they? (i) In my Adversary's cost block, or (ii) in another cost block.
4. Alternatively, what ideas are there to grow the Adversary's company's turnover line?

It goes without saying that the more financially meaty the ideas are, the easier it will be to convince someone who is on the fence about Win-Win.

Thanks to the answers to these questions, you will have identified at what level the Mutual Wins will materialize and their value. Remember the example in Chapter 2.2 where we identified a commercial Mutual Win that would look to reduce an Adversary's stock holding, and thereby their cash flow. While stocks and cash flow might be critical KPIs for a commercial leader, they certainly will be for a finance leader, or general management.

This brings us to reason #3.

3. Get to the Right Level.

As we saw earlier, it is vitally important for a successful Win-Win negotiation to involve stakeholders at the right level in both companies.

It is easy, or at least easier, to convince an Adversary of the merits of Win-Win if they themselves—not just their company—win personally. Everyone is human.

Accordingly, the Win-Win convincing has to be done at the right level. If that level is above your pay grade, as they say, then go to your boss, or your boss's boss, to ask them to do the convincing to their counterpart in the Adversary's company.

This is another reason why you need to have already gone through the first two steps, as you will be required to explain your plan to your hierarchy, including:

- The Win-Lose stakes of the negotiation, at face value, particularly if your company has much to lose!
- The Mutual Win(s) you have identified to mitigate these stakes.

My experience tells me that this presentation to your hierarchy will be seriously appreciated. It will demonstrate your ability to think outside the box, proactively plan and put the company's interests first. So, go for it!

It is at this stage that you will know how to proceed.

If you have the power, you can impose your Win-Win point of view, at a time of your choosing.

If you don't, you need to get your Adversary on board.

You may have your own tried-and-trusted method of convincing someone of your arguments. Personally, I am a great fan of the *Yes Staircase*.

THE YES STAIRCASE

The Yes Staircase is a simple questioning method that requires little practice and is, in my opinion, flawless if done correctly.

If you are unfamiliar with it, here is how it works.

Often you cannot just ask a complex, controversial question which gets you to your outcome straight off the block. In a nutshell, you require a 'Yes, I'm interested,' or 'Yes, I agree,' or simply 'Yes!' as an answer to your question.

The problem is that if your Adversary's answer starts with a 'No' you have nowhere to go. To repeat or reformulate the question is to suggest somehow that your Adversary has not properly understood it. As far as your Adversary is concerned, you've asked the question, the answer is 'No,' and that's that. That is why I would advise against this gung-ho approach.

With the Yes Staircase, you break the big question into a series of smaller, less controversial questions, which follow logic to get you to your preferred outcome. Each question must be a yes/no question, where you simply ask for them to confirm their interest to move up to the next step on the staircase.

With each 'Yes' answer, you move up a step and onto the next step, where you can ask your next yes/no question. In this way, you never move back down the staircase (after all, your Adversary has just said 'Yes' to that question)—you can only either move up, or stay on the same step. As each question is relatively simple and requires a yes/no answer, formulate it in such a way that the only professional answer is 'Yes'.

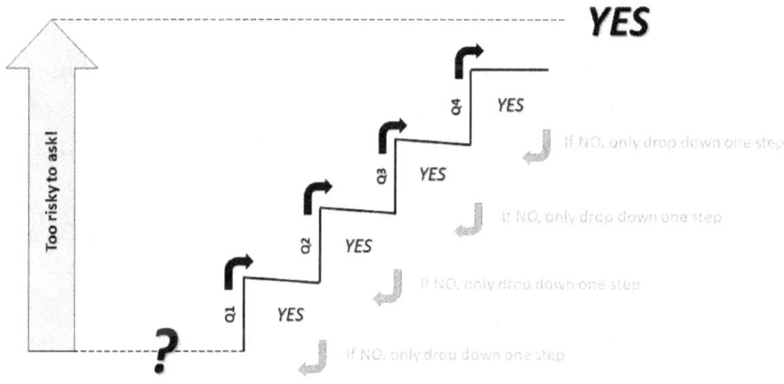

Figure 2.5.1: The Yes Staircase

If at any stage your Adversary—genuinely, for whatever reason—says 'No', then stay on that step. Do not move. Remind them of their 'Yes' answers to all the questions that got you there.

By doing so, you will remind your Adversary of the legitimacy of your current yes/no question. If you had a 'No' answer to your question, try to rephrase the question in such a way that the only legitimate, professional answer is 'Yes'.

Continue up the Yes Staircase until you get to the top! Your desired outcome.

Don't worry, there need not be many steps to the top of the staircase. The key is to ensure that you get a 'Yes' answer to them all.

Lastly, choose your vocabulary wisely. In your questions, mix up the *I*'s, the *we*'s, the *my company*'s and the *our companies* to build affinity and the notion of partnership.

Here is an example.

Let us stick with the scenario in Chapter 2.2 of a commercial discussion, where the Mutual Win is in another business area or P&L cost block—say, logistics. You want to explore ways to reduce their stocks and cash flow, rather than fight it out on price.

Instead of asking the question directly, imagine a five-step Yes Staircase...

Q1: I read recently that cash flow was one of the biggest issues that most companies are facing. Is this topic important to your senior management [or 'to you', if you are speaking directly to senior management]?

Your Adversary's answer could be 'No,' but it is highly likely that the finance director or managing director would agree that cash-flow issues are important.

Q2: So presumably, if my company could come up with ideas that deliver significant cash-flow improvement to your company, would your senior management be interested?

Same comment as above.

Q3: In the event that there were two options on the table, I presume that your company would go for the option that delivered the best result for the P&L?

Ditto.

Q4: So, in other words, if the best of these options was one that was based on cash-flow improvement, rather than, say, another one based on a reduction in another cost line, then this would be something that we should seriously explore together. Would that be fair to say?

If you get a 'No' answer to such a question, try probing your Adversary as to why such an idea should not be explored. This could also be your rephrasing angle in such an event.

Q5: With your approval then, I would like to work up a series of different options, beyond the obvious commercial ones, that will improve your company's P&L. Are you on board?

I put it to you that this offer could hardly be refused.

Accordingly, if you get a 'Yes' answer, then the door to presenting your Mutual Win is open. Bingo!

This is not the only way to get to the same outcome. Let us take a different four-step staircase to get there.

Q1: Thinking ahead to our upcoming commercial discussion, I was planning to look at ideas that will help improve your company's overall P&L. Am I on the right track?

There is a chance you could get a 'No' to this, but if that is the case, turn the question into a negative. Why wouldn't it be on the right track?

Q2: If there was an idea that meets this brief, but falls outside our direct commercial playing field, I was planning to incorporate it into the options for us to discuss. I presume that this would be fine for you and your senior management?

Here, while it might not be vital to your Adversary, the key is to insist on involving their senior management. They could not really say 'No' to such an approach.

Q3: And if in this option we can go even further in driving P&L improvements for your company than our commercial topics, I presume that this would be acceptable to you and your senior management?

How can your Adversary say 'No'?

Q4: If in doing so there was a way for my company to benefit at the same time, I am sure you will find no objection?

If your Adversary responds negatively to this question, ask why there is an objection. Even if they insist, I would frankly go ahead anyway. There is no reasonable justification for you not to go ahead based on where you got to at the end of Q3!!

Thus, if you get a 'Yes' answer to this last question, the path is clear. Bingo!

As a general reminder, if you get a 'No' answer at any stage as you go up the Yes Staircase, remember that you simply go back to the last question (or step) and:

- Remind them of the 'Yes' answer to the last question, and that
- The current question is the logical, rational next step on the very same topic.

An important factor in the questions you choose is that you feel comfortable with the approach you take, such that you are confident not only in the response to the questions but also in the manner that you can insist on, and stand by, them.

In summary, it is quite legitimate that you should not be expected to know whether your Adversary is on board with the notion of Win-Win.

However, if you have identified where the power lies, done your homework on potential Mutual Wins and ensure that the Win-Win conversation takes place at the right stakeholder level, there is no reason why you should not get their approval to put your Win-Win ideas on the discussion table.

2.6

CATEGORY MANAGEMENT: MUTUALLY WINNING

Key Takeaways

1. Category management is an example of a collaboration between supplier and retailer on Win-Win.
2. There are roles and responsibilities that are incumbent on any category captain that must be fulfilled.
3. Becoming category captain brings balance between the two parties. This should be reflected in the Equilibrium Point of your Win-Win-Win Pyramid.

You may well be familiar with the concept of category management.

Wikipedia[1] tells us that 'Category management is a retailing and purchasing concept in which the range of products purchased by a business organization or sold by a retailer is broken down into discrete groups of similar or related products; these groups are known as product categories (examples of grocery categories might be: tinned fish, washing detergent, toothpastes).' This is not what I am referring to.

Instead, I am referring to the retail (or consumer goods, in my case) meaning of category management. Here, a consumer-goods retailer, such as a grocery retailer or DIY chain, identifies for a specific business category (such as toothpastes or yoghurts at a grocery retailer, or hand-tools or lighting for a DIY chain) one supplier (often the outright leader in the category) to collaborate with them on the development of the category as a whole.

The supplier, who is often referred to as the category captain, works hand-in-hand with them on every aspect of the business category with the shared objective of growing the category's turnover.

Growing the category's turnover is in the interests of both parties. If the category turnover grows, it is more than probable that the supplier's turnover as category leader will grow. A Win-Win.

As a great believer in Win-Win, I can only speak very highly of my own personal experience of category management. It is a perfect example of a Mutual Win.

While there may be certain specific KPIs that relate to certain specific categories, these shared objectives can be summarized as follows:

- Grow the turnover, and profitability, of the category by
- Growing the number of product purchases (e.g. from 1000/day to 1010/day)
- Growing the average basket of products (e.g. from 2.3 to 2.5)
- ... And thus grow the profitability of the category.

Becoming a category captain does not mean that better commercial terms need to be given, or should be expected, by either party. It places a customer/supplier relationship at a completely different level.

In fact, one could argue that once you become category captain, you should no longer treat your counterpart as an Adversary, a term that I have used throughout this book.

They become your partner, or even your ally, although I wouldn't go as far as the latter!

There is a responsibility on the category captain to behave with complete objectivity in all category matters, once appointed. This point must be taken seriously as it might mean that:

- On the basis of factual sell-out data, you must accept that a competitor product is listed in place of your own.
- You must sanction activities that are implemented by your competitors, rather than those that you might have proposed for the same time slot.
- You have to integrate competitor launches and innovations as they come forward, potentially at your expense.

Retailer and category captain pool category insights, on consumer profiles and behaviours, for instance.

Lastly, from personal experience, being category captain is an extremely time-consuming activity and most probably will involve having team member(s) dedicated to nothing else.

If you are unable to accept the above, then do not become a category captain.

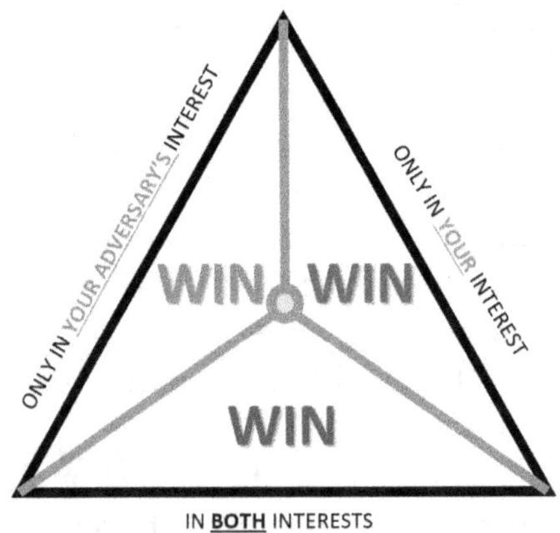

Figure 2.6.1: Equilibrium Point in Category Management

If all this sounds interesting, then category management is as good a Win-Win as it gets.

Becoming category captain has an automatic impact on the Win-Win-Win Pyramid. The Equilibrium Point will move from any unbalanced position that you might have identified beforehand to a more balanced one (see *Figure 2.6.1*).

Being category captain, in this respect, takes off any immediate pressure that you might feel regarding commercial terms—always a sensitive subject between the two parties.

That said, the pressure intensifies on the category captain elsewhere. A category captain will be expected to walk the walk and talk the talk:

1. In putting any Win-Win ideas that you might have recommended successfully into practice.
2. In coming up with new ideas for the category as you move forward with the category management process.
3. In animating the category as new events and innovations are implemented for the benefit of the category.

In all respects, category management is a perfect example of a Mutual Win. If relevant, it can be proposed as an idea for a new Mutual Win, even with the most virulent of Adversaries.

It is a relationship game-changer.

2.7

PREPARING FOR THE NEGOTIATION

Key Takeaways

1. Be prepared to compromise in any negotiation. Establishing whether both parties are committed to finding an agreement will support finding these compromises.
2. Identify what your best alternative to no agreement will be to establish your negotiation limits.
3. Involve your hierarchy as part of your preparation for a negotiation. Align on the objectives and the potential outcomes.

As I mentioned at the start of the book, this is not a book about negotiation strategies. A negotiation-strategy book would probably cover top tips such as how to:

- Create a good first impression
- Listen, listen, listen
- Use your body in a negotiation
- Read body language
- Influence your Adversary,
  to name just a few.

Nonetheless, we need to cover three topics that are fundamentally important in your preparation for any negotiation to help find common ground that will lead to an agreement.

1. Compromise:
'Where there's a will, there's a way.'

A negotiation would not be a negotiation if there was no compromise. Be prepared for it.

Make sure that your hierarchy understands what compromise might look like, so that you can conduct your negotiation with the full confidence of your hierarchy behind you.

Confirm that your Adversary understands this. As I stated right at the start of this book, I am not an expert negotiator, in the Turkish, carpet-selling sense of the term (no offence meant as to the negotiating prowess of any reader who happens to be Turkish, or a retailer of carpets, or both!).

I am not someone who thrives on a negotiation along the lines of:

Buyer: How much for this carpet?

Seller: 1,000₺ [Turkish lira].

Buyer: What? I'll give 200₺.

Seller: 600₺. It's my last price.

Buyer: I can't pay more than 300₺.

Seller: 450₺, as you are the first/last client of the day [depending on the time of the negotiation!].

Buyer: OK. I'll give you 350₺, but it's my very, very last offer.

Seller: 400₺?

Buyer: Done. It's a deal!

As a negotiator, I do not believe in:
1. Starting ridiculously high (as a seller) or low (as a buyer).
2. Saying things that are patently untrue.
3. Using arguments that lack professional credibility.

Alternatively, I am a great believer in the expression 'Where there's a will, there's a way.'

The spirit of this expression within the context of a negotiation is to establish in a completely transparent manner, from the outset, whether there is a genuine will on the part of your Adversary to find a mutually agreeable outcome to the topic at hand.

Once established, you can confirm that you share the same will. Both parties, if they respond in good faith, have confirmed that the will of both parties is to find a mutually agreeable solution.

Now, both parties must work to find the *way*.

This approach is particularly relevant, in my view, in
- A pitch environment, where you are down to a final round of negotiations
- A salary discussion, for a new role
- A negotiation with an Adversary with whom you have a long-standing relationship and a mutual respect for one another.

'Where there's a will, there's a way' means that if both parties confirm their *will*, then both parties <u>will</u> find the (mutually agreeable) *way*.

Inevitably, it should be expected that you will not get the outcome that you would ideally like. It may well be less for you. Your Adversary will not get the outcome that they would equally like. It may well be less for them.

A commitment to this expression tacitly confirms that all parties are prepared to consider multiple options to get to the conclusion—in other words, an agreement that both have committed to.

On a human level, both parties are unlikely to feel any resentment to one another as they explore these options to the final agreement.

Unproductive personal feelings, like resentment, should be avoided at all stages in any negotiation. They can cloud judgements and lead, objectively and/or factually, to worthy topics being overlooked.

If you discover that during discussions on finding the *way*, your Adversary is demonstrating bad faith or unproductive behaviours towards an option you put on the table, then you should bring your Adversary back to the starting point. Namely, the mutually agreed *will* to find a solution. Remind your Adversary that the reason for tabling this option was in the spirit of finding the *way*.

This is respectful compromise.

2. Best Alternative to No Agreement

The best alternative to no agreement (BATNA) is self-explanatory. If you have no alternative plan should you completely disagree, you had better find an agreement! Your negotiating position is not strong. If there are several alternative options, then it is stronger.

This subject is an integral part of the balance-of-power topic that we have considered on several parts of the journey so far.

For the sake of consistency, let us continue with our commercial discussion for (say) the price of an article between a buyer and seller.

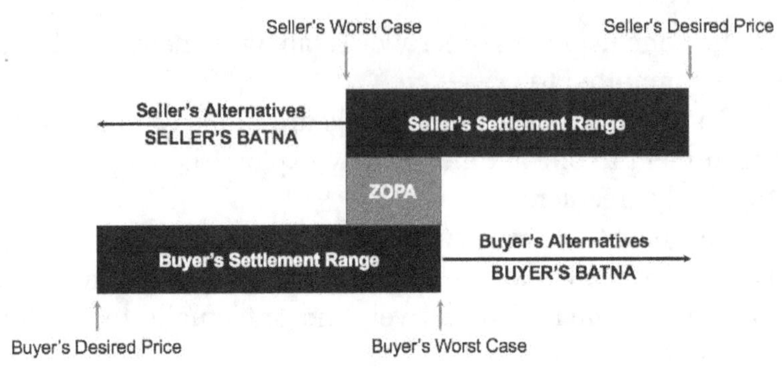

Figure 2.7.1: Negotiation Positions[1]

The diagram above (*Figure 2.7.1*) aims to capture visually the stakeholders and their two positions.

At the top, we see the seller's position. At far right, we have their *desired price* and *worst case*. The seller needs to find a mutually acceptable agreement somewhere between the two. This is the *seller's settlement range*.

At the bottom, we see the same elements viewed from the buyer's perspective. This gives the *buyer's settlement range*.

The *zone of potential agreement* (*ZOPA*) is the area that falls in both the buyer's and seller's settlement ranges.

Once you get outside the ZOPA and into each party's BATNA, the situation becomes more complex and tense. A situation where there is no agreement is potentially on the cards. Alternatives, new options, different ideas are required.

It is in the BATNA that we need to put our creative thinking caps on. It is most probably in the BATNA that Win-Win has a role to play, particularly Mutual Win topics. Mutual Win topics often explore creative ideas that facilitate getting to an agreement.

Understanding each of your own parameters will give you a full awareness of the stakes of this negotiation and, thereby, greater confidence as you move into the negotiation. In the above example, this hinges on the price of an article.

In real business life, any negotiations you face might be far more complex, with multiple parameters and a number of different variables.

Figure 2.7.1 gives us a sense that there are limits. For both parties. In some negotiations, one party can decide to walk away. The conditions are unacceptable. Your Adversary is just going to have to find an alternative partner.

Use your Win-Win-Win Pyramid to avoid this scenario. Keep in mind the saying that there is no taste in nothing. If either party walks away, both parties will end up with nothing.

You should not necessarily be pushed into accepting a bad deal that takes away from your business rather than adding to it. But if creative Win-Win solutions can be found that increase the zone of potential agreement, then both parties would be foolish to walk away from the discussion table.

But if this is not possible, fair enough! Walk away. *C'est la vie!*

However, there are many negotiations where an agreement must be found. This could be for many reasons. For instance, if you walk away and if:

- You lose this major customer, where the current cost structure of the company can no longer be supported.
- You do not get access to this product, a component part of a bigger project, then the project itself could be in jeopardy.
- There is not sufficient time to find an alternative, then the whole project timeline can be in jeopardy. This delay could have a further negative impact on other dependent projects that are in the pipeline.

All of these considerations must be run up the flagpole.

Using these parameters, together with a robust, comprehensive negotiation preparation process based on

the Win-Win Win Pyramid, will help to:
1. Increase the zone of potential agreement.
2. Provide proactive options that can be taken out of the kitbag if you find yourself in the best alternative to no agreement zone.
3. *Pre-align with Your Hierarchy*

Any negotiation, particularly a complex one where the stakes are high, be can conducted serenely and confidently if objectives, strategy and limits have been pre-aligned with your boss. Incorporate into this briefing on strategy your Mutual Wins, including any financials or metrics that support your strategy. Use the Win-Win Win Pyramid, if you see fit, to support or endorse your approach.

At the same time, agree with your boss the frequency and basis on which you should keep him/her informed of progress.

Stick to what is agreed during this pre-alignment.

During the negotiation, if there is any deviation from the pre-aligned plan, bring it to his/her attention. This will be your opportunity to revisit any pre-aligned parameters.

It would be ill-advised to diverge from the pre-aligned plan without sign-off from your hierarchy. Firstly, because you cannot be 100% sure that you have authority to do so. Secondly, because you will always be more effective in your negotiation when you know you have the full support of your boss. Lastly, your boss might have an even better idea for the next step than you, thanks to their broader experience and, perhaps, access to information on other parts of the business that fall outside your responsibility.

The diligent preparation of the negotiation is a key determinant of the negotiation outcome. It should not be underestimated.

To quote the old adage, 'By failing to prepare, you are preparing to fail.'

Don't!

LOSING

Key Takeaways

1. You cannot expect to win every time.
2. Avoid resentful and bitter feelings towards your Adversary if you lose.
3. Learn from losses. Use this knowledge to ensure you win next time.

It would be unreasonable, unrealistic and unprofessional to write a book about winning without having a chapter, albeit brief, on losing.

It is also unrealistic in a career to expect to win every time and to never lose. One could even argue that in order to fully appreciate the joys of winning, one has to lose.

Make sure you win more than you lose! But there will be losses.

In a game of football (or soccer, for those reading the book in the U.S.), you win if you score more goals than you let in: 1-0, 2-1, 5-3.

There are few games where a team does not let in a goal, and even fewer where they win emphatically 8-0!

Negotiation is an everyday part of business life. There are some roles, for example in sales, where you may even negotiate several times a day.

A good day, therefore, is realistically a day where you

win, say 3-2. A very good day is where you win well, 4-1.

Letting in a goal, in other words losing one negotiation, is invariably going to happen. Don't go into a tailspin if it does.

Make sure you score more goals each day than you let in, such that at the end of the day, the week, or the month you win, despite the odd loss along the way.

If you do suffer a loss, avoid getting resentful or bitter.

Become more determined.

Learn from the losses.

Identify where the negotiation went wrong. Use your preparation time for the next negotiation, or next time around, to ensure you have incorporated the learning into your strategy. It will stand you in good stead. This is particularly important when you are dealing with an Adversary with whom you have multiple, or repeated, negotiations.

Take the wins and the losses with the same level of humility. *Every dog has his day!* In the business world, fortunes can turn quickly.

If you lost today, ensure that you win tomorrow.

This approach brings us back to the topic of resentment. Resentment and bitterness have no place in any potential professional relationship, as I have repeatedly stated. Neither do they have any place at work.

Like a sneeze, resentment can be contagious. It should not be propagated by anyone.

I am reminded of an experience where I was accompanying an independent business expert I had recommended to one of my top (and most challenging) customers, a firm that was facing serious motivational and negative employee behavioural issues. When the CEO asked for the expert's frank and straight-talking view on this employee behaviour, the expert, in no uncertain terms, drew the CEO's attention to the harsh, demotivating, resentful culture that was espoused by the organisation's leaders. He continued that their employees were simply mirroring this culture. These employees just responded to requests each day from their leaders through gritted teeth with the reply, 'Fu*k you very much!'

He continued that the CEO should not expect any different behaviours from anyone—employees, suppliers or customers—as long as this company culture persisted.

He concluded by reminding the CEO of the principles of Win-Win, particularly with his employees, as, in his view, it made companies more magnanimous in winning and understanding loss.

There are also scenarios where it is in your greater interest to lose, as we will see in one of our case studies in Part 3!

We have already established that no one likes to lose. So, this also goes for your Adversary. In business life, there are some Adversaries with whom you negotiate on multiple occasions.

Some of these negotiations will be more important to you than others. Some will be strategically important to you. Others will not. The ones that are strategic to you might not be so to your Adversary. And vice versa.

We have already established that inflicting a loss on your Adversary every single time might be good for your ego, but is likely to create resentment and bitterness in your Adversary.

Under such circumstances, it can be in your interest to lose, or at least appear to lose, on the non-strategic topics in order to win on the strategic ones.

Under such circumstances, it is completely legitimate to use the fact that you clearly lost in your Negotiation X in order to insist on your (winning) position in Negotiation Y.

In other words, you use the loss to ensure your later win.

I conclude this chapter with a couple of sporting quotes

from two of my tennis idols—Jimmy Connors and Martina Navratilova— from my youth. These quotes not only capture the important relationship between winning and losing, but also put the cursor exactly where it should be between the two.

Jimmy Connors told us, 'I hate losing more than I love to win.' This relationship between the two concepts is key in an overall determination to win.

Meanwhile, Martina Navratilova summed it up: 'Whoever said, "It's not whether you win or lose that counts," probably lost'!

Game, set and match to winning.

PART 3

WIN-WIN-WIN IN YOUR BUSINESS

APPLYING WIN-WIN-WIN TO YOUR BUSINESS

In this section, we will explore how you can implement the principles of Win-Win, including the Win-Win-Win Pyramid, in your business.

We will look at 10 different case studies, with different profiles.

- Seven case studies are 'external'. These relate to Win-Win illustrations that involve one, or more, Adversaries coming from different companies.
- Two case studies are 'internal'. These relate to an in-house situation within the same company.
- One case study is 'cultural'. In this example, we explore how Win-Win can be infectious in influencing the culture and employee behaviours across a whole company.

Each case study has been chosen to complement the others, although they are obviously not exhaustive.

Each case study comes from a different market sector, often from different countries, from companies of varying sizes and with different profiles.

The case studies are all real-life experiences. Not theory.

Nor are they perfect.

Where possible, the presentation of each case study is structured broadly in the same way—albeit not identically—so that you may compare and contrast what each one brings to the table.

This is how the case studies will be structured and presented:

THE STAKEHOLDER

First, we cover the main protagonist, together with a brief overview of the individual, their role and that of their company and where it is based.

THE CHALLENGE

We then describe the circumstances that the key Stakeholder faced and the challenges that they found themselves confronted with.

THE ADVERSARY (OR ADVERSARIES)

In this section, we introduce the adversarial context that the Stakeholder was confronted with. Where appropriate, we will also try to understand the situation from the Adversary's perspective.

THE MUTUAL WIN

Here we explore the Mutual Win, or Mutual Wins, that were identified during the course of the case study and the role they play in the ultimate negotiation and its consequent outcome.

WIN-WIN-WIN PYRAMIDS

For each case study, we show a visualization of how the Win-Win-Win Pyramid would, or might, have looked in order to illustrate the stakes associated with each case-study scenario.

THE NEGOTIATION AND OUTCOME

We then focus on the negotiation and the outcomes themselves. For some case studies, these are explored individually. In others, together.

KEY LEARNINGS

Each case study has been chosen to bring something different to the table. In the Key Learnings section, we pull apart the pieces of the case-study to identify what we can learn from the case study in the name of Win-Win.

BEYOND THE CASE

Lastly, we look past the case study itself and see how it can provide inspiration beyond its obvious parameters—the business sector, the market or the business size.

In this section we therefore focus on how the case study and Key Learnings can be applied in a broader context.

There are some case studies that require more flexibility than these chapter headings allow. I trust that you will forgive this creative license I have permitted myself.

As you go through each of the case studies, I encourage you to project the situation onto your own situation, your own company or previous experiences.

There may well not be an exact one-on-one replication that can be made for your personal circumstances.

Do not let this hold you back.

Enjoy!

(WIN-)NOVATION

THE STAKEHOLDER

Oscar was the national sales director of the French subsidiary of one of the world's leading manufacturers of toys and games.

THE CHALLENGE

He was charged with identifying, and negotiating, the commercial strategy to successfully launch the biggest event of the year (if not of the decade, if the company HQ were to be believed)—the relaunch of a blockbusting new toy franchise which, although known from the distant past in the French market, was still the No. 1 franchise in the home market of the group.

The commercial strategy had to ensure that the subsidiary took outright leadership, right from the launch year, in the relevant toy category, where the current franchise leader was enjoying its fifth consecutive year as category king. Oscar viewed objectively that this was an almost impossible task. Unfortunately, the group HQ was not interested in listening!

Oscar knew that the relaunch would never get off the launch pad without the major players in the toys-and-games distribution network, of which the four leading toy specialists accounted for >40% of the market. He needed them to give him the level of support that franchise leaders enjoy from Day 1 in terms of both their in-store shelf space and the space in Christmas toy catalogues.

Oscar's issue was that his company's franchise lacked credibility in the French market. Oscar needed to persuade his toy specialists to buy into the dream of the relaunch.

He needed to convince them that his franchise was going to be the No. 1 winner of the upcoming Christmas season, and that they would win at the same time! His managing director had made it quite clear that no extra financial resources were available to put extra discounts on the table in order to buy this extra in-store and in-catalogue space. All financial resources had to be invested behind creating awareness and sell-out of the relaunched franchise.

THE ADVERSARIES

The four toy specialists were the dominant force behind the toys-and-games market in France. While Oscar, and his company, enjoyed mutually respectful partnerships with each specialist, relationships were tense. His company was already the least generous in terms of commercial conditions.

- Toy Specialist No. 1 was the outright leader, with 14 large-scale toy stores in out-of-town locations in the leading cities. Relations were particularly strained.
- Toy Specialist No. 2 had nearly 180 out-of-town locations throughout the country.
- Toy Specialist No. 3 had more than 200 stores in mainly high-street locations across the country.
- Toy Specialist No. 4 was a kind of cooperative, with by far the biggest store network of owner-operated stores that were welded into the local community, particularly the pre-school and kindergarten network.

CASE #1: (Win-)novation

Despite his 10 years of experience as sales director, Oscar was dreading the presentations that he would have to make to the specialists. He had to find a Mutual Win-Win angle to get them onboard.

THE MUTUAL WIN(S)

Working with his colleagues from marketing, he convinced his marketing colleagues to reallocate some of their marketing budget away from a national campaign and into a new fund for each toy specialist for projects that would:
- Play to their individual network DNAs. In other words, with bespoke projects that would be adapted to each store network's DNA. In this way, there would be no jealousy between the specialists once, inevitably, the word got out about what the other was being offered.
- Target awareness and drive sell-out in each chain and store location.
- Only be spent if the specialist in question agreed to Oscar's franchise-leader conditions on space in-store and in-catalogue.

Specifically, the team's plan consisted of proposing to:
- Toy Specialist No. 1: A targeted cinema-advertising campaign, to coincide with the national TV campaign, in the cinema multiplex closest to each of the 14 stores— with a bespoke advert including a personalized call-to-action for each store at the end.
- Toy Specialist No. 2: An in-store discovery activity program, where paid trainers would run special bespoke events for local children every weekend in the busy run-up to Christmas.
- Toy Specialist No. 3: A massive window campaign to celebrate the franchise launch and advertise the key franchise products selected by the chain.

- Toy Specialist No. 4: A complimentary sampling campaign for local kindergartens where each store could offer a range of pre-school products from the toy franchise.
- Commercially, to top it all, Oscar concocted an extra, self-funding, year-end commercial bonus for each specialist if the new franchise took the top slot in their store network.

WIN-WIN-WIN PYRAMIDS

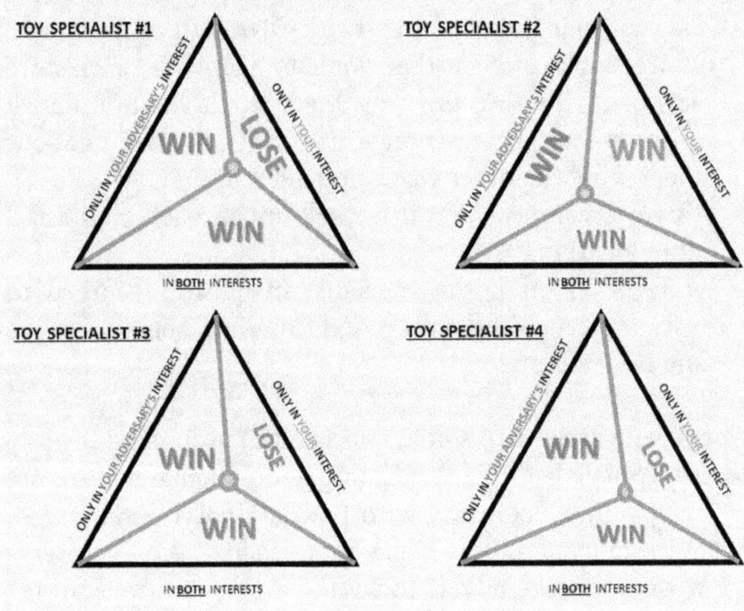

THE NEGOTIATION AND OUTCOME

The much-dreaded presentations were a runaway success. Each specialist was thrilled to have something that hit their DNA 'sweet spot'. No additional discounts had to be handed out.

CASE #1: (Win-)novation

In the spirit of transparency, Oscar also shared with each specialist what the others were getting. Each one was delighted with their proposal.

The fact that each of the specialists was getting on board in equal measures also provided each one with the assurance that, by signing up, they weren't making the wrong decision.

They were all convinced.

Commercially, Oscar and his team had played their part. Despite the standing start, the relaunch franchise would have the in-store and in-catalogue presence of a leader—at least commercially speaking.

KEY LEARNINGS

I have chosen to start our case studies with this fascinating case. Generally, negotiations are one-on-one—you against an Adversary. Sometimes, they are multiple—you against multiple Adversaries. This can be the case at the time of an important business event, such as the launch of a new product or service. In such circumstances, a single business event might trigger multiple negotiations with the same customer group on the same topic. Here, it was toy specialist retailers.

This adds extra complexity, because you cannot be seen to give to one group something that you do not give to the other. There is pressure both individually and collectively.

In this case, Oscar identified a Mutual Win based on the idea of personalization, executed according to the DNA of each of his Adversaries—the toy specialists.

This case study also demonstrates the importance of teamwork and internal negotiation. Often, marketing teams will be loath to give up valuable resources for national campaigns in order to finance specific customer activities. Marketeers feel this dilutes their national investment.

To win externally, Oscar first had to win over internally for his plan to succeed. The internal plan starts well before the external one is ready to go live. Once again, this demonstrates the importance of preparation and advance planning.

BEYOND THE CASE

There are many industries where the business calendar is marked by innovations and launches.

In this case study, the product/launch is both the pretext for the negotiation and also the springboard for revisiting the complete customer relationship. The trick that Oscar used was to combine the two.

Thanks to the complete relaunch strategy, including Oscar's commercial component, the franchise took the No. 1 leadership position in Year 1. A formidable achievement.

Oscar not only met his objectives, but also transformed his business relationship with each customer in the process. They understood that from that day on, when Oscar said they would win together, he wasn't joking!

This sort of trust is an unquantifiable trump card in any commercial relationship.

ADDING VALUE TO WIN TOGETHER

THE STAKEHOLDER

In her home country of Denmark, Mette had recently been appointed country general manager of the hairdressing division of the world leader in haircare and cosmetics. Mette's business made branded products that were exclusively distributed to hairdressing salons.

It was her first general-management role and she was determined to make it a success. She had come up through the marketing ranks and so was less familiar with some of the other important components of a general-management role, such as sales and finance.

THE CHALLENGE

Mette's biggest customer, both in terms of turnover and profitability, was Denmark's largest, and most prestigious, hairdressing chain.

The problem was that Mette's biggest competitor was on the hunt and was prepared to offer significantly higher discounts to the chain than she was currently offering.

If she matched these discounts, the profitability of her brand would take a serious hit. Her budgeted profit objectives for this year, and those to follow, would be unachievable.

Her dream of succeeding as a general manager would be in question.

THE ADVERSARIES

The hairdressing chain, founded and owned by star hairstylist Rasmus, was focused on attracting the most affluent, fashion-conscious Danish consumers and had the majority of its store locations in and around the capital, Copenhagen. The average ticket-price (the average price that each customer paid for products and services) was one of the highest in Denmark, which meant that profitability per customer was high, too.

The highest cost to the chain was Rasmus's team. He wanted to attract the very best—the best-qualified in terms of hairdressing skills, the most fashion-conscious, who dreamed of being onstage at fashion shows, and those who could offer the very best in customer service.

Rasmus's hairdressing products represented just under 20% of this average ticket price, so the choice of brand for the chain was also an important one.

He was not too dissatisfied with the product supplier he'd used for the past decade, but perhaps the recent change of general manager and the generous offer of significantly higher discounts from the supplier's biggest rival were signs that now was the time for change.

While Mette was new to sales, she was an expert in marketing. She had an in-depth understanding of Danish women's magazines and had good contacts with media leaders, particularly at Denmark's most prestigious title. Like Rasmus's hairdressing chain, the magazine targeted the most affluent, fashion-conscious women and was looking to develop its presence in Copenhagen.

Mette was also in the process of renegotiating her partnership with the title. Not only did she have discount concerns with this hairdressing chain, but she had price pressure coming from the magazine. They wanted to raise their prices for adverts.

From a profitability perspective, Mette was facing not a double- but a triple-whammy: losing her biggest customer; losing financially in her media effectiveness; and losing massively in terms of her business's profitability. The balance of power was not on her side at all!

THE MUTUAL WIN(S)

Using all her marketing experience, Mette saw an opportunity to link the two negotiations together, thereby turning her weak position with each into a strength for both.

Her two Adversaries shared the same target consumer—affluent, fashion-conscious women. Both Adversaries' businesses depended on their presence in Greater Copenhagen. Both dreamt of creating special, personal touch-points with these Copenhagen women in order to recruit them as new clients. Neither had the financial resources to do so. Both believed that the source of profitability was the creation of new loyal consumers—while keeping all other costs in check, of course.

Her Mutual Win, she decided, would be to bring the two parties together in an added-value way that had never been done before, thereby taking price—product prices for the chain, and advertising prices for the magazine—off both tables. Her key focus would be to help both Adversaries win new consumers, with a view to them growing their top-line turnover.

Her idea was to create an annual series of prestigious, fee-paying fashion shows for a maximum of 2000 consumers (400 consumers at each of the five events, she estimated) in, and around, Greater Copenhagen in an exclusive partnership with the magazine and the hairdressing chain. As part of this partnership, each would play an important part:

- Her business would pay for all costs associated with the fashion-show locations and event staging, such as lighting, catering, choreographer, make-up artists and, of course, products.
- The hairdressing chain would choose their very best team members to present on stage at their cost. They would create and choreograph the show themselves and source the clothes at their expense, too.
- The magazine would advertise each of the events for the consecutive months prior to the events, at their cost. The month after the event, they would do a four-page write-up on the event, including a two-page interview with Rasmus. All at their own cost. All of this media coverage would be strongly branded with Mette's products.
- Each consumer would receive at each show a gift bag containing products from her brand, and two gift vouchers—one for a subscription to the magazine, and the other for hairdressing services at the chain's salons.
- All revenues for the events (100 kroner per ticket, about $16) would be shared between all three parties, in the spirit of their unique partnership, in order to offset some of the costs for all parties.

She presented the plan to her boss. He loved the creativity and ambition behind the plan. If need be, it was agreed, as a backup, that her business could forgo their part of the ticket revenues (between 60,000 and 70,000 kr.) to support:

- ✓ Priority #1 the hairdressing chain—the most important stakeholder in the negotiation.
- ✓ Priority #2 the magazine—in the event that she needed to sweeten the deal.

She was ready to get started.

WIN-WIN-WIN PYRAMIDS

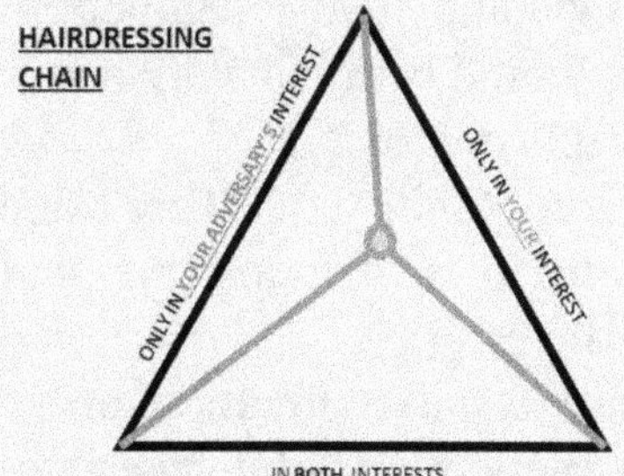

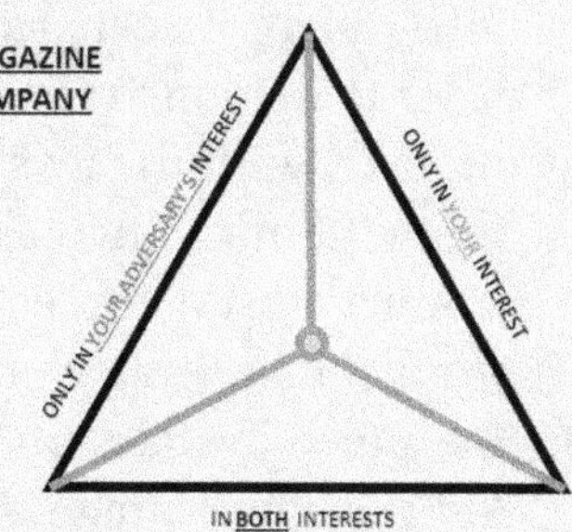

THE NEGOTIATION AND OUTCOME

Mette decided that the first negotiation had to be with the magazine publisher. She had to get them on board first.

Winning here was the key to winning with her No. 1 customer. It would also establish whether she could earmark her backup budget to her customer. As a worst-case scenario, if she lost the negotiation with the chain, she could always find other customers who would die to be part of such groundbreaking fashion shows.

The magazine loved the project. It turned out that they were looking to set up these sorts of consumer events but didn't have the money to fund them—fashion show, choreographer, location, hairdressers, clothes, etc.

They signed up, with no need to use the backup fund and no need to increase the advertising rates. The income from the events would more than cover any increase per page. They hoped that this would become a must-attend event each year in the calendars of the Copenhagen chic!

They also asked if they could do this every year!! Perfect.

Mette could now prepare for the dreaded discussion with Rasmus. It was vital that she went fully prepared. Meticulously, she put together:

1. The potential annual increase in turnover of 2000 new consumers (she already had their average service price), with different scenarios at 1500 and 1000 consumers in order to demonstrate that he would be financially better off, even with the least desirable outcome.
2. The potential increase in profitability (at the same product costs) for each scenario to demonstrate that product discounts were not the priority.
3. She added in slides on increase in staff motivation, pride, and media coverage, saving the icing-on-the-cake two-page interview with him for the finale.

Rasmus was bowled over. Never in his career in hairdressing, or 20 years as a salon owner, had he seen such an added-value project. Mette's competitor had only talked price, price, price.

The decision was easy. He was determined to sign up, without any need for further discussion or negotiation.

His chain had to be the chosen partner for the fashion shows. There was no way he wanted any of the other Danish hairdressing chains, which also worked with the same brand, being the highlight of the shows.

Mette had sealed the two deals, without negotiating prices and without the need for the agreed backup plan.

KEY LEARNINGS

I love this case study for several reasons.

It is possible to turn weaknesses into strengths. Even if it does not appear to be the case at first glance.

Companies all have dreams. Invariably, a dream is something that is beyond your means... at least today. In this example, Mette spotted that the two companies targeted the same consumer, or customer, group. She banked on the fact that, like most dreamers, they didn't have the resources to realise the dream by themselves. However collectively, by combining resources, these hopes can become a reality.

Mette had a backup plan, just to sweeten the deal, if need be. Good preparation!

Mette's Mutual Win ticked so many boxes.

Financially, it delivered more profitability (even in the worst case) than any significant increase in discounts.

From a marketing perspective,

1. The hairdressing chain could never have dreamt of (let alone funded!) the media coverage that the advertising, event feature, interview and fashion shows themselves generated.
2. Both companies had the pride of being associated with each other—the No. 1 in hairdressing and the No. 1 women's magazine title.

From an HR perspective, the events were a source of pride for her team and a motivation for those selected to be part of the fashion shows.

Lastly, the case highlights the potential dangers when key people are changed. This is an everyday occurrence in the business world. This neither means that a position is strengthened, nor weakened. It simply means that the 'relationship balls' (so to speak) are thrown up in the air. It is the responsibility of the new stakeholder to ensure that the balls fall on the strength side.

BEYOND THE CASE

In my career, I have had the pleasure of seeing this kind of case study—adding value by winning together—on many occasions.

It involves forward-thinking companies, who ultimately target the same customers or consumers, pooling their resources together to do something collectively that they could not afford individually.

There is no finer Mutual Win than this, as it pays for itself in spades, as we saw in the key learnings.

The biggest investment in Mutual Wins like this is human. It is the time that it takes to put a new idea together and make it happen. The first time around (i.e. the set-up year) always requires exponentially more investment time than subsequent years. The personal satisfaction when everything comes together, however, is immeasurable.

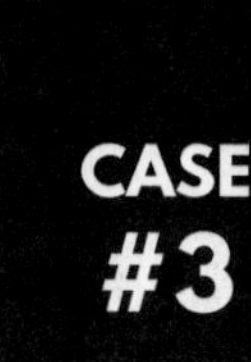

ASK, LISTEN, ACT

THE STAKEHOLDER

David had recently left one of the leading property-development companies to set up on his own. The business model of David's new company was to finance the purchase of office sites in Switzerland with the support of his investors, refit them and then lease the refurbished premises to local and international companies.

The key to financial success was getting the refurbishment done at the right price per square metre, so that he could deliver a profitable return, once leased, to his investors.

It was his first major deal. The future success of his company depended on getting everything right.

THE CHALLENGE

The office building, just outside Geneva, was now his!

The next step was to find the contractor for the refurbishment. The work needed to start in three months' time. The new tenants had to be in for September, as per the plan.

Several contractors had quoted for the complete refurbishment job. The standout quote was from a contractor who had a solid reputation for delivering a quality outcome, on time. The only issue was that the price/m^2 was significantly above the maximum David could afford.

He arranged a meeting with Alexander, the owner of the contracting firm, to discuss the project.

THE ADVERSARY

Alexander's company was well-established in the French-speaking cantons of Switzerland. The order book was in good shape, with visibility on the work schedule for the next six months.

He had quoted for the office refurbishment job for David's fledgling company. He knew of David from his days at his previous company. He would be delighted to do the job. In doing so, he hoped to become David's preferred contractor for future projects. He was confident David had a bright future.

But not at any price...

THE NEGOTIATION, MUTUAL WIN AND OUTCOME

David's objective was to reduce the price/m^2 by 20%. His strategy was to go through each section of the quote and find ways to save money without compromising on quality or time.

As things stood, his approach was Win-Lose—and it was Alexander that was going to have to make concessions (see Win-Win-Win Pyramid, below left).

The negotiation was courteous, respectful and, at all times, professional. Material concessions were made by Alexander but when David did the final financial check at the end of their discussion, there was still a 7% gap.

Rather than bringing the negotiation to an end with no agreement, David decided to give it one more try. He decided to play the honesty card, rather than a hardball take-it-or-leave-it approach.

'I would really like to work with you on this project, but

I'm afraid the price is still too high,' he said. 'How can I help you shave an extra 7% off the project?'

Alexander paused.

'To be honest, if you want to reduce the price further, I would appreciate it if we didn't have to organize all our site-installation facilities, including portal cabins, fences and changing rooms for our workforce. It is really a constraint for us and it takes me so much time to organize,' he replied.

Listening to Alexander, David saw the opportunity for a Mutual Win (see Win-Win-Win Pyramid).

David remembered that, a few years prior, in his previous job, he had been involved in the procurement and installation of such facilities. He felt it was not an insurmountable job even if it meant a bit more involvement on his part.

'It sounds like a good idea,' said David. 'How much lower could your price be if I took care of all the site-installation facilities?'

It only took a few handwritten calculations for Alexander to reply with a smile, 'If you do that, I can give you an extra 10% discount on everything else!' With that, David had a strong feeling that, even allowing for the time and costs related to the site-installation facilities, he would actually meet his budget objectives. Bingo!

In a moment of enthusiasm and satisfaction with their mutual benefit, David and Alexander stood up to shake hands to seal this double win.

On this basis, David's first project would be even more profitable than originally budgeted!

WIN-WIN-WIN PYRAMIDS

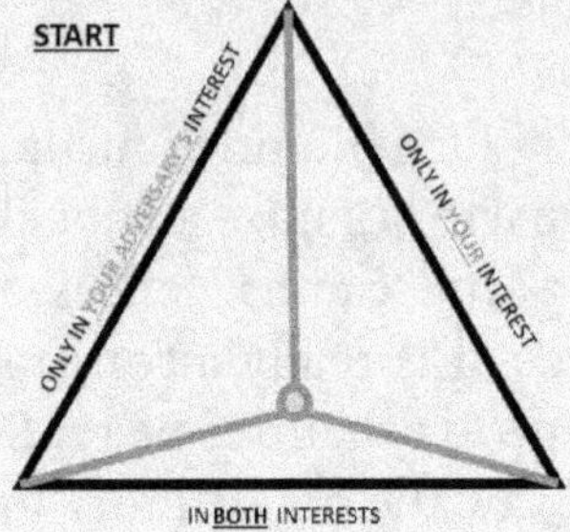

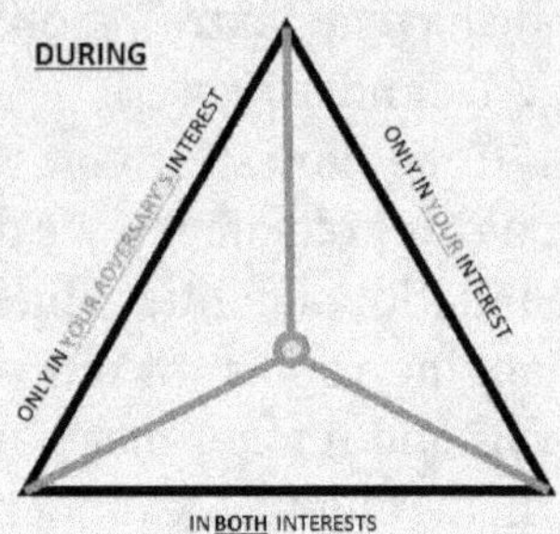

KEY LEARNINGS

The key learning, for me, here, is the human approach to this negotiation. Somewhat banally, I always say to my children that 'the nicer you are to people, the nicer they will be to you'. It's one of my values.

That does not mean that the key to success in the business world is being nice. No.

When in one-on-one negotiations, professionalism, respect and courtesy are human parameters that should never be forgotten. Under these circumstances, if someone genuinely opens up and asks if there is further scope for negotiation, you can say yes or no based simply on these human parameters.

David's approach opened a door that appeared to be closed. In doing so, he opened up new opportunities that proved to be game-changers. His honest approach led to the Mutual Win manifesting itself.

By asking, listening and acting, David ended up with an even better outcome that he originally expected.

At the same, Alexander walked away with a financially acceptable deal... and without the hassle of setting up the site-installation facilities! Win-Win-Win.

BEYOND THE CASE

I have talked a lot about the need for detailed analysis and comprehensive planning of all potential Mutual Wins. As the above diagrams show, the Win-Win-Win Pyramid on the left, at the start of the negotiation, appeared to suggest that there was little or no scope for Mutual Wins.

It was only as the negotiation played out that the Mutual Win manifested itself, as we see in the right-hand Win-Win-Win Pyramid.

This is an everyday occurrence.

I have always been told (and therefore have passed it on to my teams): 'You should never answer a question for your customer.'

When you ask your customer a question, make sure your customer answers it. Do not presume the answer. You never have the full picture of your customer's situation, so you may well be surprised by the answer.

This is exactly what happened here.

That does not mean that you win every time, but as my mother used to say to me (apologies for the series of family references in the book!), 'If you don't ask, you've got no chance of getting it.'

This also applies in business.

If you face a no-deal situation due to the scale of the Lose-Win on the table, by asking for an alternative Mutual Win then maybe—just maybe—a deal can be found in another way.

PICKING UP THE PIECES OF A BAD DEAL

THE STAKEHOLDER

Patrick had recently started in a new role as sales and marketing director of a Belgian medical supply company, specializing in orthopedic implants and a wide range of medical instruments. He reported directly to the CEO, who was also relatively new to the business.

Four years before, the company had bought an industrial manufacturing site from their biggest customer, an American firm, which, as part of the deal, agreed to exclusively source products in these two market segments for their EMEA businesses.

Today, the American company represented more than 50% of Patrick's turnover.

THE CHALLENGE

When reading the contract that had been agreed by the two parties four years ago, you didn't have to be a commercial, or medical, expert to realise that the American company had signed up to a very, very bad deal for them.

The American boss who signed the deal had now left the company. His successor was having none of this. It was just a bad deal.

Patrick now had the invidious task of negotiating a contract renewal, which inevitably would be worse for his company or mean they faced losing their No. 1 customer, with all of the structural cost consequences that go with it.

Replacement-hip prostheses were a low-added-value, high-volume item but with high profitability. Instrumentation was strategic to his company's five-year plans. Although instrumentation operated currently on low volumes and was less profitable, it was an added-value segment with significant growth potential in terms of turnover and profitability.

... In simple terms, he was between a rock and a hard place!

THE ADVERSARY

When Jim arrived as business unit head, virtually everyone he spoke to in his EMEA organization bad-mouthed their relationship with their 'exclusive' EMEA supplier from Belgium. 'Too expensive' (true, Patrick agreed), 'poor service level' and 'worsening product quality' (not true... but such was their negative perception of the supplier!).

In Jim's view, the contract had clearly been approved by idiots (maybe that was why his predecessor had been asked to leave the group?). Their company was expecting the same levels of service that the business had enjoyed before the transfer of hands of the production facility. This just wasn't happening.

The hemorrhaging had to be ended. There was no time to waste. If needed, they would source via their U.S. or Asia supplier.

He summoned Patrick to inform him of his decision to potentially bring their partnership to an end.

THE MUTUAL WIN(S)

At face value, things could not have been worse.

The message from the Americans was clear: *You have made a fortune out of us for the last four years; now it's our turn!*

It was obvious that significant reductions in price would have to be given, and, considering the animosity expressed by Jim, there was going to be no room for discussion.

No room for talking about Mutual Wins. It was take it or leave it.

Patrick knew the American company well. In fact, 10 years previously, he had worked for them! He knew their culture. He knew the determination of senior management when their minds were made up. He knew that the replacement-hip prostheses were highly strategic to them. He knew how he would have reacted if he had been in their shoes: the same way.

The strategy, as Patrick saw it, was to break the negotiation into two parts.

In the first negotiation, he would discuss the replacement-hip part of the deal—the part that interested them the most—in order to demonstrate that he understood the urgency and the importance of this element of the business to them. He would suggest that they got the new deal up and running, then attack the second phase a few months later. With the balance of power so clearly against him, there was no chance to find a positive outcome on prostheses. He knew the prices were going to have to drop—by as much as 20%.

In the second negotiation, they would agree terms on the instrumentation part of the business—less important to the Americans, but of strategic importance to him. At this point, he calculated, the balance of power would shift in his favour. A productive and appeased negotiation was potentially feasible. This would be key. Given that the instruments business was strategic to his own company, Patrick wanted to:

- Negotiate the prices up, not only to compensate for the concessions he would inevitably have to make in the first negotiation, but also to
- Help improve the midterm profitability of his company
- Improve the logistic terms (MOQ, lead times, delivering quantities, etc.) in his favour.

Patrick aligned his plan with the CEO and agreed his negotiation limits for the replacement hips.

WIN-WIN-WIN PYRAMIDS

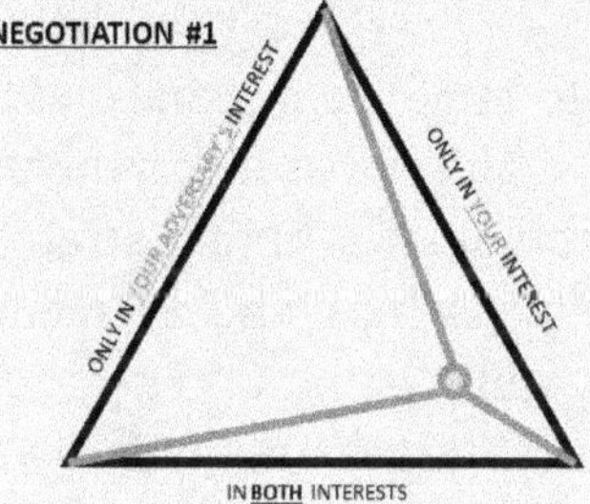

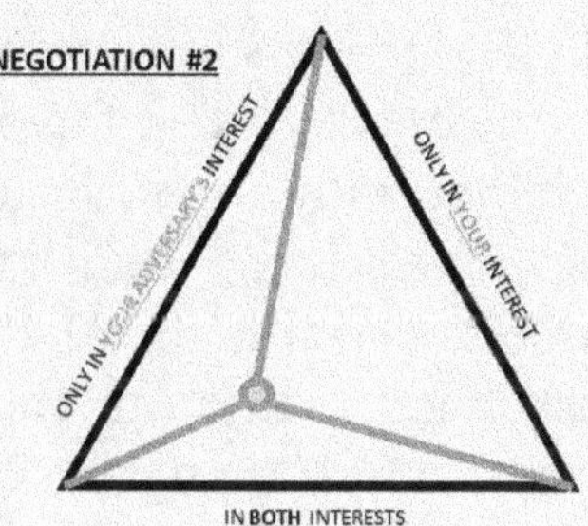

THE NEGOTIATION AND OUTCOME

Patrick managed to convince Jim that they should talk before stopping their working relationship outright. He appreciated the idea of splitting the negotiations into two parts:

1. The easy, quick, important part for the replacement hips, and then
2. The longer part for the range of medical instruments.

Serious price concessions had to be made—a bit more than was agreed with his CEO—and supply service levels agreed between both parties for the next three months. His CEO agreed to the proposal. Part one was over.

Over the next three months, Patrick followed service levels to ensure that all agreed levels were met. Emotions moved from outright animosity to demanding, yet respectful. It was time for part two.

The improved climate between Patrick and Jim allowed for a constructive discussion. Jim was clearly less concerned about these products. He admitted that Patrick had made significant concessions on the replacement-hip prices and so was prepared for an upward increase in the medical instruments against the same logistics terms.

In fact, given that Patrick had conceded more than originally planned in part one, he cleverly added in an extra 3% increase, on top of the increase he had originally planned, to offset the loss in margin!

The final act of part two was to bundle parts one and two together with a new, balanced, volume-based partnership incentive scheme. Under the scheme, if separate stretched targets were hit for a) replacement hips and b) medical instruments, the Americans would gain an extra cash bonus, which would be comfortably self-financed by the increased margin in volumes.

Part two was signed off. Patrick had successfully avoided a crisis, significantly minimized the 'penalty' that his company had had to pay for the bad deal that had been made four years prior, and also built a new Win-Win era in their cross-Atlantic partnership.

KEY LEARNINGS

When I first heard Patrick's real-life experience, I was really engaged.

As I mentioned earlier in the book, one of the reasons why the strategy of 'I win big-time, you lose big-time' does not work in the long run is that it builds up negative emotions such as resentment, bitterness and, sometimes, hatred. Often, as long as the same stakeholders stay within the business, it is possible that the only thing that will change is the cumulative increase in these emotions over time.

As soon as someone new comes on board, the first thing they will do is find a way to break the deal. I am sure you have overheard comments like, 'Can you believe this deal?', 'Only an idiot would have signed it,' 'I knew from the outset that this deal was wrong.' This is exactly what I'm talking about.

So, the first key learning is to never let yourself get into this position in the first place!

The second is that if you are the one, like Patrick, who is forced to take the brunt of a resentful Adversary's ire, then take a leaf out of Patrick's book:

- Break the situation into its component parts.
- Identify where you can 'get' (if possible) to compensate for the 'give'.
- Put a strategy together that manages not just the business.
- Align everything first with your boss!

Another learning is that the balance of power, the Equilibrium Point, can often move from one side to another. In my experience, poor service levels are one example of the parameters that can very swiftly skew the balance of power. Unless you work in supply chain, this may well be beyond your power.

That said, use those variables that are in your power to move the balance of power—the Equilibrium Point—in your favour. Invariably in business, you only have one shot at presenting a project, scheme or idea to someone, so make sure the timing is absolutely right. Choose a time when the Equilibrium Point is optimal.

Lastly, by choosing the right moment, you will most probably find that your Adversary is more open to creative Mutual Win ideas. Be prepared to wait for the right time, particularly if the topic is strategic.

Remember, Rome wasn't built in a day.

BEYOND THE CASE

This is not a case study about winning in the face of adversity. It is about:

1. Dealing with the face of adversity, with a level head and good preparation work.
2. Ensuring that you do your best, with the aim of coming out of it stronger than before.

I am sure that we can all think of situations where a bad deal suddenly falls under our watch.

Next time, you will either have to fix it or find yourself in the firing line of a seriously and justifiably upset Adversary. I hope this case study will have provoked you and will help you pick up the pieces of a bad deal, too.

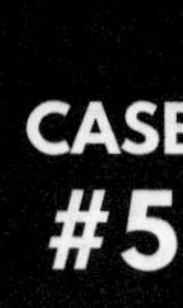

(WIN-)WINNING NEW BUSINESS

THE STAKEHOLDER

Cédric and Olivier were successful insurance brokers. Although their business was performing well year-on-year, both had ambitious growth plans for the business.

Winning new business was a key component of their strategy. Rather than targeting small-bit customers, their targets were big-budget customers, where the competition was fiercest and inevitably the sales conditions extremely generous.

This did not daunt them. They were both young, dynamic and prepared to think outside the box.

On top of that, they both loved the challenge!

Cédric and Olivier identified car-fleet insurance as a good place to start.

There were several local companies with significant car fleets, and car-fleet insurance was a sector that traditionally generated long-term repeat business.

So far, so good....

THE CHALLENGE

Cédric and Olivier knew the car-fleet insurance space well. It was a traditional sector of the business, in the respect that the rules of the game were the same for everyone.

Businesses needed car insurance. Insurance brokers had access to the full range of insurance products offered by insurance companies, which they would, in turn, propose to these businesses.

The insurance brokers would be paid exclusively via a percentage commission from the insurance company for the product that the business would sign up to. There was neither a transactional flat fee nor any additional commission between their company clients and the insurance broker.

These simple rules meant that the only way to prize companies away from their existing insurance brokers was to accept ever-decreasing commissions from the insurance companies.

A Win-Lose, if you like. Cédric and Olivier were sure that there had to be another way.

THE ADVERSARY

Arthur's company was a well-established player in their business sector, with a significant number of sales representatives that visited their customers each day. Each sales representative had a fully serviced company car.

As finance director, Arthur was responsible for the car-fleet insurance and enjoyed a good relationship with their current insurance broker.

He knew the rules of the game. They paid a fixed fee to insure each car, no matter whether there were any claims against them. Additionally, there were the hidden variable fleet costs which included the excess associated with each claim, the cost of a temporary replacement car, the lost sales of rep downtime and, and, and.... These hidden, variable costs often had a significant impact on the total cost of running the fleet.

The company had a large car fleet and was largely

satisfied with its insurance broker and fleet insurance policy. In Arthur's eyes, there was no urgency to change suppliers.

That said, the phone call that he had just had from Cédric and Olivier, insurance brokers whom he did not know, had left him somewhat curious.

He decided to meet them to understand more.

THE MUTUAL WIN

In looking at the traditional car-fleet insurance model from all sides, Cédric and Olivier felt that there was something inherently not right. There seemed to be an insufficient financial incentive or win for companies, even where claims were low. At the same time, traditional insurance brokers had little reason to bring this to the client companies' attention as they were paid a percentage commission for each car. It was a gravy train. Both insurance company and insurance broker gained when the insurance premiums went up. The only loser was the client!

They saw this as their opportunity. They would turn the tables.

In changing the rules of the game, they identified a new Mutual Win by creating a new possibility for a company like Arthur's to win. And the insurance company wouldn't even have to lose, as their net revenues would not be affected!

Their idea was simple.

They would renege on their commission from the insurance company, thereby making the car-fleet insurance less expensive per vehicle. Instead, they would agree a flat fee for each insurance claim that would be paid by Arthur's company. This fee would be set at a level that would cover their internal costs for dealing with each claim, and leave them with an acceptable profit at the same time.

A Win for them, too.

As part of their pitch, they would recommend a full package of actions for all car-fleet stakeholders in Arthur's company to reduce the number of annual claims.

They believed that Arthur's company would see a significant annual reduction in the total cost of running the car fleet. To demonstrate their confidence and the transparency of their approach, they would also ask for a (fair) share in this reduction—say 20%—as a bonus fee. No savings, no bonus. Big savings, a bonus.

When preparing for the pitch to Arthur's company, Cédric and Olivier calculated that Arthur's company would have to have a seriously high level of claims to end up paying more in total tomorrow than they were paying today.

They were ready for the meeting with Arthur... and confident of the outcome.

WIN-WIN-WIN PYRAMID

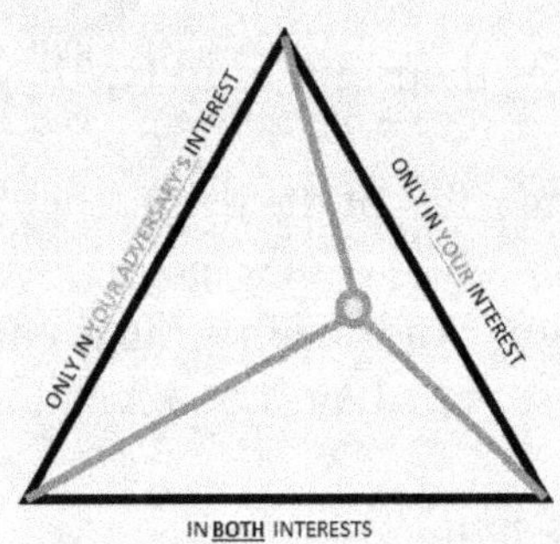

THE NEGOTIATION AND OUTCOME

The key to the negotiation was to get Arthur to agree that:
1. His company was interested in paying less in total to insure its car fleet (a no-brainer!), and that to do so...

2. He was prepared to look at a new, different way to pay for car-fleet insurance and manage claims (a bit trickier!).
3. He would share any reduction in a fair way with the insurance broker that could make it happen.

By using a questioning technique similar to the Yes Staircase that we saw in Chapter 2.5, Arthur could only agree to the first question, could have no reasonable way to say no to the second, and could barely say no to the third.

Cédric and Olivier were now ready to present their complete proposal, including its Mutual Win.

Once presented, Arthur had a simple choice to make:
A. Stick with business as usual and have the comfort of knowing that the total cost for their car-fleet insurance 'was what it was'. No change. A passive attitude.
B. Alternatively, change the rules of the game, gaining a materially strong chance that total car-fleet costs, including direct insurance premium and other associated indirect costs, would decrease, based on their claims history and the package of claims-reduction actions. Change. A go-for-it attitude.

Which option would you go for?
Arthur decided to give Cédric and Olivier a try.

KEY LEARNINGS

In this case study we see some of the topics that we have already covered in the book.

Once again, we see the importance of quality preparation. In fact, we see it in every case study.

Next, we learn the vital importance of getting your Adversary to buy into the concept of Win-Win. The questioning technique that Cédric and Olivier used was key to this.

Without the simple questions, the chances of success would have been far slimmer, relying on the hope that the idea was of interest to Arthur. Thanks to these important questions, Arthur (unknowingly?) opened the door to listening to an alternative to his current way of doing business. Assuming that Arthur was sincere in his answer, the chances of a positive outcome became exponentially higher.

By thinking outside the box and identifying a new, different model for car-fleet insurance, Cédric and Olivier crafted a Mutual Win that otherwise would not have existed.

It was this Mutual Win that enabled Cédric and Olivier to win over an Adversary who, at the outset, was not even looking for a change of supplier.

Then there is the bonus fee. On the one hand, this fee provides extra revenue for Cédric and Olivier. Fair enough! The key point for me is the fact that this bonus fee is a perfect mechanism to spotlight the Mutual Win and demonstrate their confidence in their proposal. If their proposal did not bring any savings, they would get nothing. If it did, they would get something. In my experience, this example of putting your money where your mouth is sends a perfect Win-Win message.

Lastly, I am also convinced that the creativity and determination that Cédric and Olivier demonstrated in their approach will stand them in extremely good stead with Arthur's company to take on some of its other important insurance contracts in the future.

BEYOND THE CASE

Winning new business is the lifeblood of any company.

If your company is not working on projects to win new business, then your company is going backwards! Not even standing still.

That is because your competitors are most probably swooping around your customers, as you read this book, with a view to poaching their business away from you.

Here we see Win-Win as a powerful, if not determinant, tool to help win new business.

In this respect, this case study, I hope, should strike a chord with everyone.

No matter the size of your business. No matter your role in the business you work in, think about what outside-the-box ideas, based on Mutual Wins, you can develop.

Share these ideas with colleagues. As your idea is outside the box, they may have a contribution to add that will take it even further... or, alternatively, less far. This can happen, too. In any event, nothing will have been lost.

Once these Mutual Wins have been identified, proactively look for a mechanism, like the bonus fee, that links both sides into the Mutual Win. Do not be shy in doing so. After all, if you can bring to someone an idea that will deliver them a saving of (say) 100, they will probably be happy to share 20, or 10, with you! This what I would call the icing-on-the-cake negotiation. Once you are at that stage, you will know that you have won their business.

Yes! Win-Win *can* help you win new business.

**CASE
#6**

A MARKET RESET, THANKS TO WIN-WIN

THE STAKEHOLDER

Paul was the president of sales and marketing, Europe, for a market-leading manufacturer of prestigious, high-end cameras. In their home market in Germany, the brand was a household name—synonymous with cameras that took unrivalled photos. Sales were growing year-on-year and profitability was high.

They had adopted the same key success factors in their sales and marketing strategy across the rest of Europe, but the results were more than disappointing. In certain markets with significant business potential, such as France, the United Kingdom and Italy, the business was caught in a vicious circle.

Something had to be done.

THE CHALLENGE

In Germany, the company's cameras were the favourite brand for both professional and amateur photographers. The cameras had retail prices that were significantly higher than those of their competitors, but the quality of the cameras' photos was unrivalled, too. From a commercial perspective, the brand enjoyed a broad distribution, principally in specialist photography stores. Part of their success they attributed to the fact that retail price cutting was not allowed—under any circumstances. After all, their cameras were the finest on the market.

This same commercial strategy had been implemented across other European markets. Broad distribution across photography specialists; retail prices in line with those in Germany; no discounts. The issue was that, while their brand renown helped guarantee wide distribution across 600 specialist stores in France, for instance, the average retail sales per store were a fraction of those in Germany.

In a nutshell, the business was going nowhere. Paul's company was dissatisfied with the situation; his customers were dissatisfied with the situation too.

To make matters worse, the firm's distribution base in many markets was so broad that they just didn't have the financial resources to invest in a meaningful turnaround solution; and Paul's CEO made it quite clear that he should not budge one jot on their retail pricing and commercial discounts strategy.

A full market reset was needed. But how?

In the absence of any internal inspiration, Paul reached out to a sales and marketing consultancy for insight on how to get his company out of this Lose-Lose situation.

THE ADVERSARIES

In this case, there was no single Adversary.

For each market, there was simply a collective of potential Adversaries—all photography specialist retailers. Some specialists were more virulent than others. Some specialists had significant growth potential. Others, less.

Retail prices were invariably the biggest issue, but Paul knew that this topic was not up for debate.

THE MUTUAL WIN(S)

With the brand's clear position on pricing understood, Paul and the consultants worked on a four-pronged reset strategy:

- Firstly, the consultancy team conducted a situation analysis and market-potential review in order to identify a reset strategy that could first be tested in one well-chosen EU market before a pan-European reset rollout would be implemented later, subject to its success and key learnings.
- Next, they brainstormed around all of the specialist touchpoints and consumer touchpoints (excluding price discounting!) in the total-sales process—from the product leaving their warehouse to the final consumer purchase. They particularly focused on the touchpoint variables that were in the mutual interests of both the brand and its customers.
- Then, they conducted a thorough review of the distribution to evaluate those specialists, where their price was going to be an insurmountable issue, either for them or their customers.
- Lastly, for the remaining customers, they quantified the support they could afford to extend to each specialist in order to step-change their commitment to the brand and their levels of retail success per door.

No stones were left unturned. There were no holy-cow topics that could not be discussed.

As a result of this process, France was identified as the test market, and two radical decisions were made to underpin the reset strategy.

- The first decision was to move from a broad distribution to an exclusive one. For France, this meant drastically reducing the number of distribution points from 600 to less than 50, thereby allowing them to focus investment resources.

- The second decision, for these 50 remaining customers, was to put together a personalised added-value support package for every customer that would help explain the multiple competitive advantages of their cameras, in order to justify the brand's premium retail-price positioning. Staff training and in-store consumer events would be the two focus areas:

1. From a training perspective, a brand-new package for customers' sales staff was designed. In it, staff would be proactively (and simply) trained on how to ask a consumer, in a leading way, what quality of photos they were looking for. If the consumer answered that they were looking to have top-quality photos, then only one camera brand (theirs) would meet the requirement! Simple...

2. In terms of consumer engagement, the team also devised a number of informal in-store event formats, for both professional photographers and amateur enthusiasts— the key consumer stakeholders. The objective of these events was to enable these vital stakeholders to come to the stores and witness these competitive advantages themselves.

One of the additional advantages of this selective distribution strategy was that it further endorsed the company's policy on retail pricing. By drastically reducing the distribution base and playing the exclusivity card, the potential ability of consumers to play one retailer off against another virtually evaporated. Retailer profitability would be more ring-fenced and predictable, thanks to the reduced consumer pressure on retailer-driven consumer incentives.

The final touches to the new strategy were signed off by the CEO. Paul's team and the consultants were ready to move forward together on the implementation phase.

WIN-WIN-WIN PYRAMID

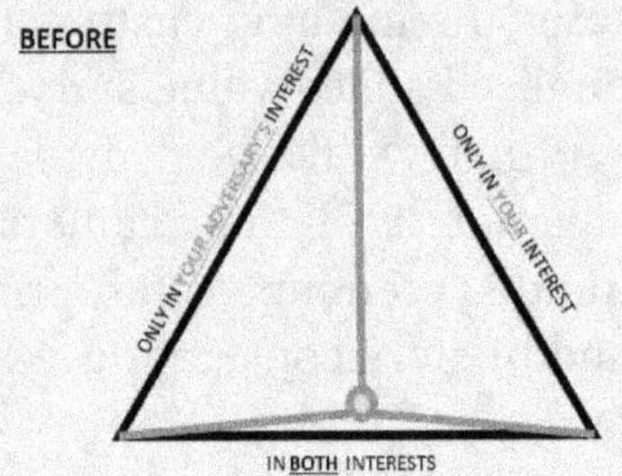

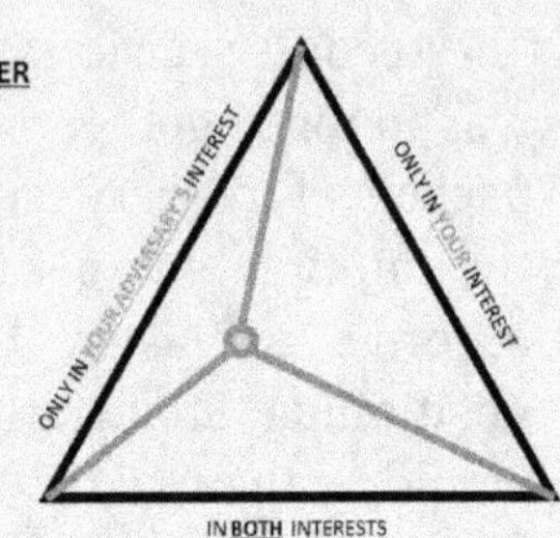

THE RESET ROLLOUT

For the 50 chosen future partners, personalized presentations were made to each customer, with major focus on the added-value training and consumer-engagement packages. These customers not only appreciated the new, highly selective approach in the brand's distribution strategy, but also the broader benefits of having better trained and motivated staff members to support the sales of all their products, not just cameras, across their store. No other camera brand took this approach.

For all the other customers, annual commercial contracts were not renewed. Their commercial relationship was brought to an end.

THE OUTCOME

Following each customer training, the reset strategy started to pay off within a matter of months. Sales per door increased significantly.

Each in-store consumer-engagement event was also a revelation. Professional and amateur photographers appreciated the added-value, intimate approach of 'seeing is believing'. With the sales discussion having moved from price to quality, selling these high-priced cameras became significantly easier overnight.

Within two years of the reset, the turnover generated by the 50 selected specialists equalled that of the 600 specialists beforehand! In Year 3, the brand went back into growth mode for the first time in years.

The reset test was a success.

The rollout to remaining European markets could go ahead at full steam.

KEY LEARNINGS

In this case study, we see three new important dimensions to Win-Win.

The first is price. In most commercial relationships, price is the most obvious (and frequently the most important) component. Invariably, if a retailer, for instance, is not selling a product at the anticipated levels, their recommendation to their supplier will be to reduce the retail sales price by reducing their purchase price proportionally. But what if the supplier refuses to countenance such an idea, either for reasons of principle or price-harmonisation across multiple markets?

The result is commercial deadlock (as we see above, in the 'before' status of the Win-Win-Win Pyramid).

The second is scale. In previous case studies, we have been able to put a name, or a face, to Adversaries. At the heart of our examples so far, there has been a one-on-one relationship or negotiation. Here, we have a case study on a different, bigger scale. We are looking at a complete market.

Win-Win as a concept, and the Win-Win-Win Pyramid, are both applied at a higher, more strategic level. Adversaries cannot be identified qualitatively. They are analysed quantitatively.

The same Win-Win principles apply, nonetheless. If deadlock is to be broken and price must be removed from the table, then identifying (i) Mutual Wins, and (ii) those customers for whom these Mutual Wins will be of interest, is potentially the only way forward (as highlighted in the 'after' status of the Win-Win-Win Pyramid above).

In this instance, we saw the combination of staff training and targeted in-store consumer events as the Mutual Wins. The former is a frequent source of Mutual Wins, and an effective tool to step-change results and any business relationship. It should never be underestimated.

The last new dimension is outside support. A fresh pair of eyes brings a fresh perspective. In this instance, the company sought outside support from a reputable consultancy company. Thanks to the outside unbiased view, a market-reset strategy could be concocted that fully respected the red line on retail pricing and discounting.

BEYOND THE CASE

Businesses that operate across multiple geographies will invariably find that their results vary from market to market. Sometimes markets can be clustered according to the business results or characteristics. At some point, strategies in these markets will need to be revisited and, in many cases, reset.

For markets that disappoint, a Win-Win approach, often based on 'more from less', as we saw in this case, is one of the best options to pursue.

Accordingly, when there is Lose-Lose deadlock and a full reset is required, looking for Mutual Wins across the full value chain and touchpoints can turn defeat into victory.

If you are in a business where foreign subsidiaries are performing satisfactorily, do not disregard using this approach. In this instance, you will have the enviable challenge of taking the markets to the next level. An identical Win-Win approach can be the ideal strategy to accelerate development in these well-performing markets, too.

In these markets, such is the level of success enjoyed by your customers that price is not a sensitive topic for discussion, either. The same strategy we saw being rolled out in terms of training and consumer engagement can also apply.

As market results are good, it is quite likely that the financial resources to invest in these Mutual Wins will be more abundant. These Mutual Wins could be used to increase distribution, either in terms of number or the quality of the doors. Instead of a more-from-less approach, in these circumstances, more-from-more could be a winning approach.

Lastly, in this case study, we have seen how Win-Win can operate on a macro level—across markets—in your business, not just on a customer (or micro) level.

Indeed, for any business that operates globally or across multiple countries, taking a one-strategy-fits-all approach is extremely problematic. Continents and countries often have completely different distribution models. Cultures vary from one country to another. Consumer behaviour, too.

There is inevitably the need to maintain variations in your strategy in order to cater for some of these differences. In our information age, retail pricing is one of the parameters in a strategy that must remain fixed. It cannot be compromised.

This case study eloquently demonstrates how this parameter can indeed be fixed, while allowing a local adaptation for other parameters—in this case the distribution policy—to support the well-known notion of 'Think global, act local'.

BETTING ON THE FUTURE, TOGETHER

THE STAKEHOLDER

Basil had decided to set up on his own in the event-organisation business, having gained more than a decade of experience in the sector in various management roles. He had identified that there was an opportunity to create a brand-new trade event in the freight-transportation sector. He felt that the needs of this growing sector were not met by existing trade events.

For his idea to be realized, he had to find a venue—a key success factor for any event. The more prestigious the venue, the easier it would be to attract companies in the sector to participate. Freight transportation should not be an exception to the rule.

Basil knew the management team of the most prestigious U.K. event venue well. He knew the prohibitive commercial conditions—price/m² of event space, upfront guarantees, minimum participant commitments, payment terms, calendar slot—of an unproven event from an unproven fledgling company. Only fully established, renowned event organisers had the clout to negotiate significantly more favourable terms. His personal relationship with them was not going to be enough. Business was business, after all.

He understood that his new company simply couldn't

afford anything like these conditions or any of their demands.

THE CHALLENGE

The negotiation situation he was facing (see the Start Point in the Win-Win-Win Pyramid below) was looking completely implausible. Whichever way he turned, his negotiation strategy wasn't going to work. He had no negotiating power. There were no Mutual Wins that he could see.

A different, less prestigious, venue was not an option. It was the key to the project's success. He had to come up with a new plan.

He decided on a different strategy that would require two negotiations, not one.

Step 1: Negotiate a comprehensive partnership with a leading event organizer that:
- Was not operating in any remotely competing freight or transport markets.
- Could (virtually) guarantee him affordable trading terms and a calendar slot.
- Would give him access to all its back-office functionality and services.

It would obviously come at a price, in terms of autonomy and share of the prize, but it was the only way of achieving Step 2.

Step 2: Once secured, the next step would be to negotiate with the event venue together, led by his new event-organisation partner based on their current trading terms.

Basil recognised this strategy would take longer to implement, but he calculated:

1. It was the best way of ensuring that his new idea would get off the ground.
2. Financially, he would be better off giving up a part of the winnings of the project, than not having anything at all. There is no taste in nothing.

That is, assuming he could pull both steps off...

THE ADVERSARIES

Step 1: The Event-Organisation Partner

Sarah was the managing director of one of the U.K.'s leading event organisers. The business was entrepreneurial at its heart, with a wide portfolio of events across the U.K. and the globe. Her business enjoyed the very best trading terms with even the most prestigious event-venue companies.

This portfolio approach allowed her business to have a broad mix of events—across industries, in growth vs. in decline, U.K.-based or international, short-term vs. long-term.

Step 2: The Event Venue

Bill was the commercial director for the U.K.'s most prestigious event venue, in the heart of London. It was his responsibility to ensure that the venue had a full calendar of diverse, profitable events... that would be repeated year after year.

He only had a small commercial team, so it was important to choose event organisers who had a broad portfolio of annual events. His team had neither the time to deal with small players, nor the financial capacity to take the risk on them.

WIN-WIN-WIN PYRAMIDS

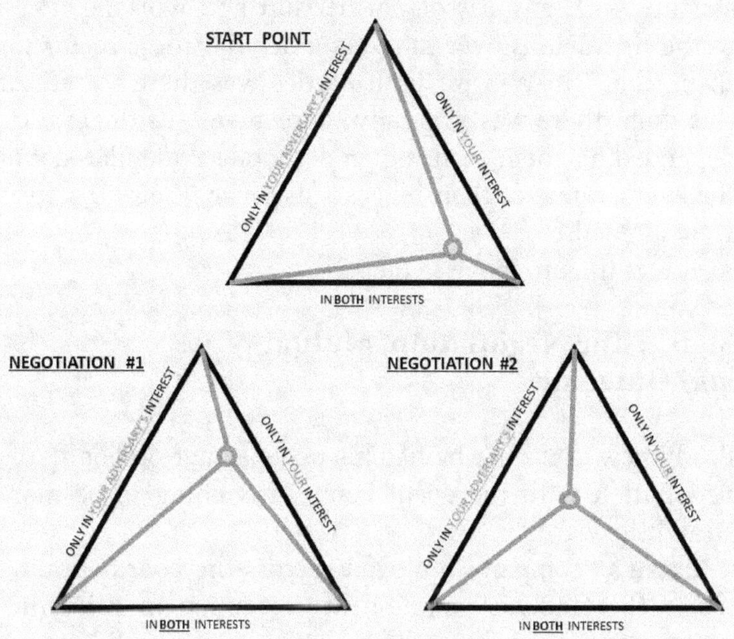

Step 1: The Negotiation, Mutual Wins

Basil's plan consisted of going to one of the U.K.'s biggest event organisers and offering them a long-term partnership in his new event.

His new project represented a fresh opportunity for each of them. It would be a massive Mutual Win for them both, if successful.

Additionally, this new opportunity would not need any extra back-office resources, an important cost-driver. So even in the (unlikely) case of a failure, the event organizer would not be out of pocket.

Before meeting Basil, Sarah did her homework on him. He had a good reputation in the industry. He was recognised as a talented professional. He could be trusted.

The negotiation went well, over a number of meetings, starting with a spirit of partnership and working down to the fine details over time. As a new business sector for them, the Win-Win for both parties was there to see. At this stage, there was a tentative agreement—its finalization depended on them securing an acceptable calendar slot at the event venue of their biggest customer. Their objectives were aligned.

It was time to move to Step 2.

Step 2: The Negotiation, Mutual Win and Outcome

Basil knew that once he had his new partner on board, the negotiation with the event venue was going to be more straightforward.

Sarah's company enjoyed across-the-board trading terms that included significant discounts on prices/m^2, preferential payment terms and no preconditions or minimum guarantees. Their buying power was considerable. The balance of power was in their hands.

Sarah took charge of the meeting with Bill. In imperial style. Basil was there simply for the idea pitch for his event. As far as Sarah was concerned, the calendar slot was a formality. It had to be found.

As a new business for everyone, she positioned Basil's event as a Mutual Win for everyone. She insisted on a special Win-Win-Win pricing scheme for this new business opportunity, comprising:

- Even better prices for the startup phase, years 1 to 3, in order to support startup investments on their side for marketing the event.
- Prices in line with current terms for years 4 to 7.
- Higher prices, in other words with lower discounts, for years 7 to 9.

- A return to the across-the-board prices from Year 10 onwards.

In other words, Bill's company would be expected to support a strategy for success at the start, in order to reap the financial benefits significantly once the event was well-established. After all, success was in all of their interests.

The plan was bold, coherent and innovative. The common thread was the long-term success of this new event. The short-term risks were limited, the long-term payoff significant.

Deal!

THE OUTCOME

The three parties agreed the detailed terms of the agreement, based on Sarah's guidelines. A mutually acceptable slot was found in the venue's calendar that coincided nicely with the seasonality of the business.

Today, the event has passed its 10-year anniversary. All three parties have gained handsomely from the project.

Won-Won-Won!

KEY LEARNINGS

There are a number of key learnings to take away from this case study.

As the expression goes, if at first you don't succeed, try, try, and try again. But in the business world, unfortunately, when you present a new project to someone, you often only have one shot! So make sure you get it right first time. This is exactly the approach that Basil took when it came to securing one of the key success factors of any trade event— the venue.

Having analysed the situation from all angles, he realised that, by going it alone, he wouldn't be able to pull it off. It was mission impossible!

The project represented his future prosperity. For it to fly, he needed to find a strong business partner, a leader in the same event-organisation sector. Even if it meant teaming up with a (potential) competitor. David would team up with Goliath!

It was the power of this combination that created the momentum for success. Thanks to Basil and Sarah's partnership, the impossible mission was transformed into a far more straightforward customer-supplier negotiation.

The biggest key learning is the Mutual Win. The future is often the most powerful Mutual Win.

Negotiations frequently get bogged down by the short-term worries of today or tomorrow. By getting your Adversary to focus on what mutual success looks like in the mid- to long term, you can often ease tensions over short-term concerns. As you have an aligned vision of the future, a solution to short-term topics can more easily be found.

In this instance, the event venue gave up something more in the short term so as to support the prospect of gaining more in the longer term.

Lastly, there is the universal key learning that, in the business world, everyone should at all times manage their reputation. Reputations, in my experience, take a long time to build and a short time to lose. Reputations cover relationships with all the stakeholders that an individual interacts with during their career—up or down, internal or external, competitor or customer. Reputations often dictate how someone will listen to and appreciate a new business opportunity.

It is my firm belief that someone with a reputation for Win-Win will have a better ear and a more objective appreciation of a new business proposition from an

Adversary than someone who is renowned for Win-Lose.

BEYOND THE CASE

This case study perfectly illustrates the power of new business.

New business is an obsession in business today. If that is not true in your business, then I would recommend you make it so. This case also illustrates the creativity that can be brought to the table when it comes to new business. Rules are less defined and can be reinvented or adapted. We saw good examples of this in this chapter.

This case study speaks out, beyond the example per se, to the small that have big ambitions. These ambitions can be realized, but, as we saw here, finding allies to strengthen your position is often the difference between winning... and not winning.

Lastly, there are some business sectors and industries that are more focused on the long term than others. If you are working in such an environment, I hope that this case study will give you serious best-practice food for thought.

If you work in a more short-term sector, or industry, this does not mean that a Mutual Win based on the future cannot, or should not, be explored.

Far from it.... It simply requires you to more forcefully put forward the arguments for agreeing what mutual future success would look like. The Yes Staircase that we saw in Chapter 2.5 can be an effective tool to get your Adversary to open up to your proposal.

CASE #8

WINNING... IN UNION

THE STAKEHOLDER

Thomas was the newly promoted human-resources director of a key division of a major French utilities group. There were more than 10,000 employees in the division, spread throughout the globe, but the vast majority were in multiple locations in their home market, France. The firm was in serious transformation mode. It was moving away from their traditional core business of heavy-duty electrical cabling and into modern electronics. This meant that the employee skills required in the past were not the skills needed in the future.

Thomas had a comprehensive and qualified HR team. He was proud to say that his team were genuine business partners to each business function, the unions and other workplace bodies.

Thomas's boss was the group's chief human-resources officer. Although she strongly supported him, she expected Thomas to hit the ground running in his new role. She expected results.

THE CHALLENGE

As human-resources director for the division, Thomas was the figurehead in the relationship between the group and its *partenaires sociaux,* the unions. Many companies in France have had the reputation of poor them/us relationships with their unions. Conflict can be frequent. Systematic opposition to change is often widespread. Constructive cooperation on strategic HR topics is sometimes lacking. Trust can be in short supply. Sadly, Thomas's business was no exception to this picture.

From a turnover perspective, the business transition from electrical cabling to electronics potentially offered extremely positive perspectives for the division. From an HR helicopter view, this was also positive. There was work to be had for everyone.

That said, for this potential to be realized, the business needed to adapt to different skill sets and have greater geographical mobility as they moved through each step of the business transformation process.

The challenge for the division was to manage this transition seamlessly, without friction or employee conflict. If the employees embraced these changes, everyone could win. If they did not and chose opposition, or strike action, not only would the financial costs to the business be massive, but also the division risked completely missing a smooth and successful trajectory for the transformation.

As the elected representatives of the employees, the union representatives from the three leading unions held the key. Thomas's boss made it clear to him that the future success of the division was in his hands.

Thomas had two strategically key agreements that he needed to negotiate with the unions in the coming year.

The first would address location-based employment issues. As the business transitioned, certain functions in certain locations would suffer business impacts. Some of them would take time and so were difficult to perceive from one day to the next. Others were sudden, such as the loss (or gain) of an important contract. Where the impact was swift, the relevant operational teams could give real-time updates.

The second agreement was linked to the first. It was the topic of *next-step skills training*. As the transition worked its way through the business, affected employees would not only have to be trained in the new skills, but also have to consider moving to different group sites. All of this could only happen with their understanding and cooperation.

Thomas was seriously feeling the pressure!

THE ADVERSARIES

Each of the three leading unions had a union representative. At face value, these representatives were like any other employee. They had operational roles and reported to operational line managers. Unlike other employees, though, their union responsibilities, such as employee consultation, coordination with and training by their union headquarters and, of course, discussion with the group via the works councils and other group committees, meant that they were rarely actually focusing on their operational tasks.

It was fair to say that, historically, there had been little trust between the unions and the group. There was also a certain degree of tension between the positions of each of the three key unions.

Being a union representative was not an easy task. The group was going through significant change. Like many companies, change is feared by employees.

The appointment of the new HR director was yet another change within the change. Although Thomas had a reputation as an honest, respectful HR professional, none of the three union representatives viewed this important appointment with an auspicious eye.

THE MUTUAL WIN(S)

While union representatives were often the cause of sleepless nights and conflictual workdays, Thomas had respect for them.

Their situation wasn't simple.

In terms of the employees they represented, they were the sounding board for all their grievances and could not be seen to be in the pockets of the group.

Professionally, in becoming union representatives, their career prospects disintegrated in an instant. Their line managers viewed these individuals as a headcount who didn't pull their weight in the team, despite the fact that they were paid for out of its budget. They felt that their allegiances were first to their union and not to their own operational team.

Thomas's view was that this operational setup was not helping constructive union-group dialogue. They were caught between two stools. They were 100% paid for by the operational business, but only operational a fraction of the time.

This was wrong. Changing this would be his Mutual Win.

Thomas's plan was to take the union representatives completely out of these lip-service operational roles. Instead, he would integrate them into his own HR organization as a separate HR task force, reporting directly to him and paid for by HR.

The HR task force would continue to work on all of their usual union-representative tasks—but also, as a task force, they would work both collectively and individually on strategic topics that were important to the division.

At the same time, Thomas would invest in training them to give them an even more detailed understanding of new, relevant law changes than their own union base could give them. Not only would this give them a better appreciation of the issues, but also it would give them extra credibility when dialoguing with employees and personal satisfaction at their own personal development.

Thomas's objective was that the task force would create a new middle-area—a mutual zone—in group-union relations. There would not be a 'them' or an 'us'. The task force's mission would be 'we'!

The cost would be virtually neutral to the division, but Thomas would need to get support from the group chief HR officer, not only because of the completely revolutionary way that he intended to treat the union representatives, but also as he needed to get board sign-off for moving financial resources from the left pocket (operations) to the right pocket (HR).

Thomas knew that this revolution was going to put his neck on the line. He pitched his ambitions to his boss. With a curiously raised eyebrow, his boss agreed. 'You'd better make this work!'

Now he had to convince the unions... before starting any discussions on these two strategic topics.

WIN-WIN-WIN PYRAMID

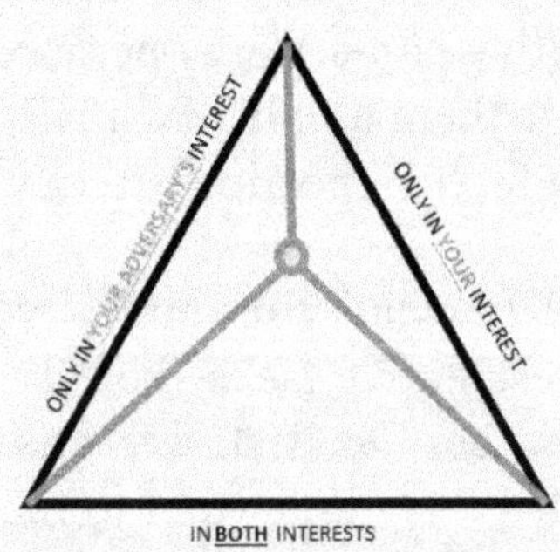

THE (FIRST) NEGOTIATION AND OUTCOME

Thomas's bold, outside-the-box, untraditional, call-it-what-you-want idea took the unions and their representatives by complete surprise.

Work in HR, reporting directly to the new HR director? Be part of a group task force working on a group project? Step out of operational roles? It was a revolutionary proposal in every sense of the term.

Relieved by the idea that they would no longer be in operational roles, the union representatives were personally seduced. They decided that they should each consult with their union HQs in order to get their feedback and, if positive, their approval.

The union HQs agreed that the new scheme could be tested out. They were still wary.

The changes were made with immediate effect. Their official union work continued as in the past, and the remaining time was then allocated to their personal development and individual and collective task-force project work.

There was a weekly one-on-one meeting with Thomas, just like with all of his other direct reports. They were to be treated in the same way, after all.

Within weeks, the union representatives were unanimously positive. At last, they felt recognised. They were working on added-value projects that were in line with their centre of interest. At least they felt as if their own resources were being used for the good of the company. Even their weekly one-to-one meetings were appreciated. Thomas treated them in the same way as the rest of the HR team. Firm, but fair.

In the spirit of transparency, Thomas had them participate in HR team meetings so that they could also understand the state of the business and the role that HR needed to play to support its development and transformation. This was an important part of Thomas's plan, too.

THE (STRATEGIC) NEGOTIATIONS AND OUTCOME

Once the new task force had settled in, Thomas set the mutually important agenda to the entire HR team for the two agreements that would have to be negotiated over the coming months between the group and the unions.

Roles and responsibilities were assigned, together with the calendar of deliverables.

From Day 1 of the negotiation, behaviours from all stakeholders were completely different from the past. Instead of monologue, there was dialogue. Where previously there would have been potential conflict, there was constructive debate. Instead of resistance, there was exchange and engagement. Trust reigned. The ambiance was not 'you' versus 'us'. It was 'we'.

Negotiations were both cooperative and constructive.

For the agreement on location-based employment issues, a cross-functional team was set up to monitor employment issues at each site and proactively alert the task force if the danger lights were flashing on workload visibility. High-risk locations were identified and a proactive plan identified for each one on the scope and scale of the potential drop in activity. The task-force members were sent out to each location in order to work closely with local teams to discuss the situation and advise them on potential solutions, including the touchy subject of geographical mobility.

For the next-step skills training agreement, the task force worked with the operational team to understand the skill-set requirements that would help experienced team members transition from heavy-duty electrical cabling to modern electronics. Subject to the issues identified in the above risk analysis, a proactive skill-set bridge was set up to prepare the at-risk team members in the designated locations to be ready to take on new responsibilities in the group, if required.

In short, both Thomas and the unions came away with vitally important agreements that they could both wholeheartedly sign up to.

KEY LEARNINGS

This is our first internal case study. One where we see Win-Win applied *within* a company and not externally between two or more companies.

In all internal cases, the notion of 'we'—we, the employees, together—is both particularly sincere and extremely powerful. In fact, when correctly and effectively implemented, we see that the 'in your interests' or 'in my interests' disappear. They become imperceptibly, 'in our shared interests'.

For internal applications of Win-Win, the we/us/together will always be a Mutual Win. Here, we see a perfect implementation of this. As a result, two strategically important topics are transformed into a collective process where the parties are no longer seated on the opposite sides of a table, but instead are seated together around the same table.

Another key learning in this case study is the power of Win-Win in cultural change. For those readers who have worked in groups or countries with a heritage in strong union activities, you know how a company culture can be determined by the relationships between unions and employers. Here, we see how Thomas's creative idea will have gone beyond these two agreements and positively impacted not only the very culture of the company, but also the regard that each employee will have towards their employer.

Thomas empowered the organization, including the

unions, to work together on mutually important topics. Today, empowerment is a term that is often bandied around too freely in organisations. Empowerment starts with words, deeds and actions from the most senior management. This is then followed up with daily activities and tasks that are completed in line with that taken by those empowered. Empowerment cannot just be a word on a PowerPoint slide.

This case study is a fine example of empowerment.

As in other case studies, we also see the significance of the notion of speed. When faced with a strategic problem, many professionals go ahead. At speed. Here, we see that Thomas paused first, by setting up the new task force, before pressing ahead on the strategic issues.

Indeed, the hare-and-tortoise analogy is probably applicable here. To go ahead directly at speed would have meant encountering, and having to overcome, multiple obstacles (hopefully!). By pausing and taking the time to embed this new working relationship with the unions, Thomas created an environment where obstacles were flattened out. When Thomas pressed the 'go' button, the path to the finishing line was unencumbered.

My last learning is one of courage. It takes courage, even more so in large multinational (often political) groups, to change the rules of the game. Thomas showed a double dose of courage. First, towards his employer, as he proposed a revolutionary change to the way in which union representatives are treated by the business. Secondly, courage towards the unions, by outstretching the same hand to stakeholders who have been often treated as Adversaries.

It also took courage from the unions themselves. Unions are organisations that are also steeped in history and traditional behaviours. While I do not know it for sure, I expect that the union representatives might have had to do a great deal of convincing to get their traditionally minded union headquarters on board.

BEYOND THE CASE

This case study is clearly relevant to big companies and ones where unions are a key agenda item. However if you do not work in either of these two environments, there is still something to take away.

Many companies are having to manage significant change. In all cases, such change cannot be managed single-handedly.

Thomas showed skills that are applicable to all companies going through a period of change—no matter their size.

He demonstrated the importance of thinking outside the box. He showed courage. He showed his company that, when implemented correctly, there can be a different way to achieving success.

Food for thought...

CASE #9

EMPLOYEE MOTIVATION

THE STAKEHOLDER

Cathy had opened her first coffee shop seven years ago. There were only four employees in the company at the start. Now, she had six shops, all in the same area within a 20-kilometer radius, and 31 employees, including in-store and back-office personnel.

Managing six shops was far more complicated than just the first one. But that was part of the job.

THE CHALLENGE

Cathy was proud of her achievements. It was a real team effort.

While she wasn't the best payer in the restaurant trade, she certainly wasn't the worst. They were in the average zone.

As the number of coffee shops increased, so her management challenges increased. Managing multiple store locations was not easy. She was determined that the teams not only delivered great service day in, day out, but that they did not lose sight of their financial targets—monthly and quarterly.

The first two quarters of the year had been positive. They were above the previous year and above budget. But, when analysing the KPIs from the first two months of the third quarter, she could not help noticing that the positive trend was plateauing. Footfall was up 1% over the period, but the average turnover per customer was down 5%. Absenteeism was up by 7% too. This cost Cathy a fortune in replacement temporary staff, as each time someone was ill they had to be replaced. Customer service should not suffer due to absenteeism.

To make matters worse, three of her store managers had come to see her in her office that day to inform her that morale was low; in-store staff were looking elsewhere, they believed. One of the managers unfortunately announced that she had had a resignation the day before. Several employees were asking for salary increases ... or else!

With rent increases on the horizon, Cathy could not afford to increase salaries, at least at this stage. Worse than that, she simply didn't have the time, or resources, to recruit several new in-store staff members.

THE ADVERSARIES

Her biggest asset, her team, which had helped her get to where she was, was potentially turning into her No. 1 preoccupation.

Cathy didn't have the financial resources to employ someone to be in charge of Human Resources. She managed it herself. Every recruitment took up the equivalent of four to five days' work, even if she delegated part of the task to the in-store managers. Not to mention the fact that she had to pay recruitment fees to the agency and, on top of that, temp-agency fees if she couldn't find someone in time between the resignation and the end of the notice period, one month later. Her team were not vindictive but she had fully understood the message from the in-store managers. She had to take the topic seriously. They were expecting a material response and they expected it swiftly.

The ball was firmly in Cathy's court.

THE MUTUAL WINS

While Cathy believed she had the power in the employer/employee relationship, she nonetheless wanted to demonstrate to the team that she took the topic extremely seriously—and professionally, too.

Each in-store employee had a fixed salary and a modest monthly bonus if their store targets were achieved. The back-office team had a fixed salary only.

Cathy decided to explore all of the Mutual Wins that she could think of. In other words, ideas where both she, the owner, and the team could win together. She penciled a few Mutual Win thoughts on paper, based on the criteria that she wanted her solution to meet:

1. All-in, all-out solution. Everyone should win together, or lose together.
2. A help-each-other-out scheme, whereby if one store was above target, they could compensate for one that was below.
3. Everything should be transparent. Where there was money to be saved, the team should benefit.
4. Self-financing. The scheme should be financed out of any over-achievement versus the budgeted targets.

She composed a list of potential solutions:
- An annual *profit-sharing scheme*, based on an over-performance against the budget
- A quarterly *turnover bonus*, based on an over-performance against quarterly cumulative company targets
- A half-yearly *loyalty bonus*, funded by the fact that there would be no recruitment fees or temp-costs
- A *cost-to-turnover ratio* bonus, to ensure that costs were constantly in check. She was open to discussing the periodicity on this one.

In fact, Cathy was pretty much open to any constructive suggestion from any employee—in-store or back-office—as long as it met the criteria of her Mutual Win ideas.

In her mind, she identified that it would be fair that any over-achievement would be shared equally between her and her employees. In other words, for every extra $10 generated, $5 would be for her and $5 would be for the employees.

As a backup, she could potentially revisit this ratio. After all, she was well aware of the benefits to her if the company hit its budgeted targets in the first place. Over-performance was extra for her, too.

With so many potential Mutual Wins, she felt confident as she went into the negotiation phase.

WIN-WIN-WIN PYRAMID

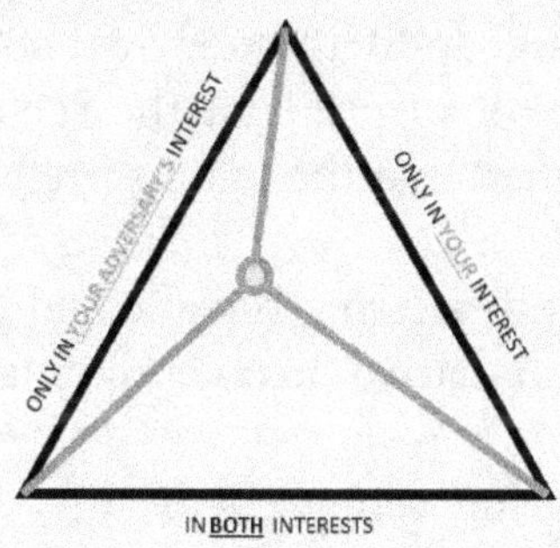

THE NEGOTIATION AND OUTCOME

There was no union representation in the business, but Cathy wanted the negotiation to integrate all of the employees. She therefore chose one person from the head office, and asked the store managers to pick four team members from different stores—two store managers and two in-store employees. A total of five. She called them the task force. The task force would speak for their fellow team members and would consult with them on each stage of the process.

She planned three meetings in total with the task force.

1. The first to present the status of the business, her Mutual Win principles, ideas and parameters.
2. The second for the task force to come back with their two preferred approaches, together with reasons why.
3. At the last meeting, Cathy would present the final plan.

The constructive approach regarding the process was much appreciated. The team felt empowered.

They appreciated the transparency with which Cathy presented the company situation, and the Win-Win spirit of the Mutual Wins. The team had heard other friends talking about some of the ideas that she was proposing, but never thought they would apply to their own business.

Much to Cathy's surprise, at the second meeting, the task force confirmed that the team's preferred two options were:

- The annual profit-sharing scheme and
- A quarterly cumulative turnover bonus.

The profit-sharing scheme was their No. 1 option, as all employees could contribute to its objectives. With the turnover bonus, only the stores were on the front line.

Cathy decided to respect the task force's No. 1 recommendation. Profit sharing it would be.

She worked on the scheme. Should it be a percentage-based scheme (i.e. same percentage to be shared, no matter the over-achievement)? Or a level-based scheme (i.e. different payout levels based on different over-achievement levels)? She opted for the former, in the spirit of simplicity and ease of understanding.

At the third meeting, she presented her proposed scheme and informed the task force that the scheme would apply with immediate effect. (She had implied in the first meeting that it would be for the following year.) Something she had kept up her sleeve! The gesture was appreciated.

The negotiation had been a success.

In terms of the rollout, Cathy announced the scheme to the head-office team and toured each of the stores directly afterwards. This was to ensure that everyone was informed directly by her, with the opportunity of asking questions at each session.

Ten days later, she organized an in-store manager meeting at the head office to get employee feedback on the scheme and learn the extent that the motivation issues they had previously expressed had been dealt with.

Although everyone would have preferred an immediate salary increase, she felt comforted to know that the motivation fire had been extinguished, for now.

The team appreciated:
- The transparency of the process
- The creation of the task force and the empowered role that they had been given
- The openness of each of the three meetings
- The fact that several options were put on the table, with the task force participating in the choice of the final, preferred option
- The communications rollout, including the opportunity to ask Cathy questions directly
- And, of course, the Win-Win approach of the new profit-sharing Scheme.

Cathy, at last, breathed a sigh of relief and celebrated with the managers with a glass of champagne.

Why not!

KEY LEARNINGS

The French have an expression I particularly like, which goes, 'Il faut être ferme sur le fond, mais souple sur la forme.' Loosely translated, this means standing firm on the end result, but flexible on the means to the end. This is exactly what Cathy did.

She was adamant that salary increases in fixed salaries were not on the cards, but that increases in remuneration by a different method were possible.

She wanted to send the message that she took the topic seriously. The appointment of the task force and the three-meeting process clearly demonstrated this.

She integrated the team, via the task force, empowering them to constructively participate in the solution.

Lastly, she ensured that she demonstrated respect to employees and clarity in the simple manner that the scheme could be explained and understood by all.

BEYOND THE CASE

I particularly like this internal case study, not just because of the outcome but because of the manner in which Cathy applied the principles of Win-Win to her business.

I have always been positively surprised at the manner in which team members rise to the occasion when integrated proactively, professionally and respectfully in the process—even in heavily unionized countries that I have known.

Win-Win has infinite applications when applied within an organization, no matter the scenario—between employer and employees (as in this case study), different teams, different stakeholders.

Beyond the Win-Win topics on the negotiation table, living by Win-Win internally is the best training tool to ensure that Win-Win is adopted across the board. Not just for commercial topics, but as a business value that pervades the whole company and its culture.

Lastly, this case study speaks volumes as we see that Win-Win can be applied to small businesses, as well as bigger ones.

In fact, internal Mutual Wins are often easier to identify and easier to negotiate, as the stakeholders know each other intimately, so to speak.

In the external cases that we saw earlier, the Adversary worked for another company. In these situations, there will always be areas of doubt, misunderstanding or uncertainty.

When applied internally, there should be none of this. This means that the scope for finding Mutual Wins is larger. There simply needs to be an alignment on both sides to explore Mutual Wins with a view to finding a mutually agreeable solution.

The company wins. The employees win. We *all* win together.

CASE #10

WIN-WIN IS INFECTIOUS

In our final case study, we will explore how Win-Win can influence company culture. I am a great believer that the difference between *good* and *excellent* in a company is *people.*

Each day, the people in any team uniquely determine the quality of their outputs. Good people who are engaged and motivated will generate *excellent* work. Good people who are not engaged and are demotivated will generate *good* work. After all, they are good people.

So, where's the difference, I hear you say? The difference lies in the company culture.

There are multiple books on this topic alone, so I will not deep-dive into this massive topic. I will simply state that:

- Company culture has a profound influence on people's performance.
- Win-Win can be used to complement a company culture and positively influence good employees to be more engaged and motivated within it.

I have personally found that when Win-Win is integrated into the way a team operates, Win-Win behaviours pervade the whole company and their actions. Assuming that these behaviours are not countercultural to the company in question, Win-Win projects bring a new dimension to everything that is great about working in and as a team.

As a means of demonstrating this, and thanking all of my team members who have been part of my Win-Win journey, I will allow myself to use some personal examples of how Win-Win has been embraced to add value in other ways than simply financial.

In each of these examples, there is of course a business (i.e. financial) part to it (after all, most businesses are not charities or non-profits!), but finance was not necessarily the be-all-and-end-all of each project. Each Win-Win project played to other components, such as:

- Employee engagement and pride
- Helping others
- Raising the flag for a cause
- Promoting the industry or a segment of the industry
- Or just being part of something bigger...

This list is not exhaustive.

In my career to date, I have had the pleasure of working for three companies, all global leaders in their fields, in three different industries.

So I have chosen to highlight one Win-Win experience from each of them.

For each of these three cases studies, there are no chapter headings, or Win-Win-Win Pyramid. They are just real-life stories—although, as a spoiler alert, I should say that one of these projects (I will not say which one) had to be cancelled on the eve of the launch date due to tax authorities who clearly weren't on the same Win-Win page as all of the other stakeholders.

Here you go...

#1: Getting Homeless Women Off the Streets

Women's underwear is a seasonal business—spring/summer collections (pinks and pastel shades) and autumn/winter (burgundy and autumnal tones). At the end of the season, there are always unsold products. Once out of season, their commercial value decreases exponentially.

After a few seasons, their market value is a fraction of the original price, but they take up the same space in a warehouse as their new-collection counterparts. Commercially, they are (sadly) virtually worthless.

From a quality perspective, they are no different to their new-collection counterparts, either. It's just that they are no longer in season.

Ethically, they cannot be destroyed. A worthy home needs to be found for these 'worthless' products—from both the commercial-value and accounting perspectives.

As managing director, based in France, of one of the world's leading brands, I challenged the team to look for worthy projects for these leftovers, or close-outs, as they are often known in the trade.

Based on a chance meeting and a TV documentary, the team understood that there were thousands of homeless women in France. The majority of these poor women lived on the streets, not in shelter homes. Living in the streets was dangerous, physically and health-wise.

A woman who goes to one of the 400-plus women's shelters in France is given a bath or shower and a health checkup. They then come on the radar, if you like.

The team proposed offering a brand new underwear set—a bra and pants—to every homeless woman in France. These products would be taken out of the aged close-out stocks and given as a gift at one of these shelters. Obviously, we hoped that the underwear set would be appreciated, but the main objective was to get the women on the radar. Safe, clean, checked up.

We had the products.

A charity specializing in the distribution of goods to women's shelters was enchanted by the idea and overwhelmed by the admirable objectives of the project.

We had found a distribution partner.

The project could not be advertised on television or in the women's fee-paying press. The project could not be called out by call-to-action in-store point of sale materials. Homeless women had no access to any of this.

Instead, we reached out to our partners in the daily free press and outdoor advertising sectors. From time to time they have available advertising space. Perhaps they could use any available space to promote the project. They signed up immediately.

We now had communications partners.

Internally, the project was heralded by all. It brought a proud smile to everyone's faces.

Thanks to our excess stock, our project to get homeless women off the streets could go live.

I haven't counted the number of separate wins in this wonderful project, but there are a lot.

#2: Giving Toys to Disadvantaged Children

The second case is similar in some respects, but different in others.

I had just joined a world-leading manufacturer of toys and games, again in France, as the managing director. I was, frankly, brand new to the company, the industry and the country.

To galvanise the team and explore their teamwork and collective creativity, I set up an internal team-based competition to come up with fresh ideas for the following year's budget—a process that would start the following quarter.

The winning team's idea would be presented to our European president and incorporated in our budget for the next year. It was a sort of internal Win-Win team competition, if you like.

There were seven fantastic ideas, but here's the winner! Les Jouets du Coeur ('Toys of the Heart').

All French people know of Les Restaurants du Coeur ('Restaurants of the Heart'). It's an iconic charity, founded in 1985 by the French comedian Coluche, that feeds France's poor and needy. Each year, the French nation is asked to offer food, household and hygiene products in supermarkets throughout France. In 2018, Les Restaurants du Coeur served 130 million meals in France. Hats off!

The Toys of the Heart team's idea was that whenever a toy was purchased in a participating store, the same toy would be offered to a disadvantaged child via the Les Restaurants du Coeur network.

The team had already identified a selection of first-class bestselling toys that would fit the bill.

Next, the team had to get Les Restaurants du Coeur on board. Their management was convinced of the genuine nature of the project and its laudable objectives. They agreed not only that we should proceed, but also that they'd use their iconic logo, replacing the word *restaurant* with *toy*, to help give us extra credibility.

Next, we had to get the distribution onboard, including toy specialists and the grocery trade. Commercial partners who signed up would simply have to find demonstration space for the impactful point-of-sale displays the team had created to celebrate the event. I am proud to say that there was unanimous sign-up.

Lastly, the team wanted to make this a whole-company initiative. They presented the entire plan to the employees and, with tears in their eyes, asked everyone to raise their hand if they were prepared to volunteer to help in one of the Les Restaurants du Coeur soup kitchens. There was not one single person who didn't immediately raise their hand with pride.

Toys of the Heart was a downright success and I suspect that, like me, the rest of the team regarded it proudly as one of the best team projects they'd had the pleasure of being associated with.

Everyone was a winner!

#3: Bringing Beauty to Job-Seeking Women

I was working in the hairdressing division of the world's top beauty and cosmetics giant. When you work in these circles, fashion shows and glitzy launch events in splendid locations are part of daily life. At the events, women across the globe are celebrated. Top models. Top designers.

We all felt so lucky to work in this environment. This was our day job!

Sadly, for many women, life is very different. Many are out of work, applying for jobs and hoping for that chance to get an interview. Often, these women don't have the means to get themselves—their hair, makeup and nails, for instance—looking great for that decisive, all-important meeting.

The team created a program to do just that.

We had plenty of products that we could make available free of charge.

The team recruited hairdressing clients to volunteer their salons and their staff.

The team then found makeup partner brands to provide their products.

Job-seeking women were invited to reach out to our company, and we coordinated the rest.

Participating salons were given impactful window communication and in-store point of sale materials to advertise the project locally.

No questions were asked afterwards as to whether the person had got the job. It was just the team's and our project partner's pleasure to help their personality, skills and experience shine through at the interview.

Getting that job would have been the icing on the Win-Win cake!

BEYOND THE CASE

The reason for sharing these cases is to encourage you to adopt Win-Win as one of the pillars of your everyday working behaviour and, if you are in a position to do so, to make Win-Win one of the key components that demonstrate the culture of your company.

When up and running, Win-Win, and the actions associated with Win-Win, become infectious.

Team members feel empowered to work in such a way.

Win-Win, and in particular Mutual Wins, often require creativity and teamwork, as we saw in the previous examples. I put it to you that all of these behaviours are fundamentally important in any successful company. In any company culture.

So, Win-Win projects such as these are worth it! Not in a financial way. Money, turnover, profits were not the prime motivators.

The reward came from the Win-Win environment—yes, the daily Mutually Winning environment—that was created around them.

PART 4

CONCLUSION

NO MORE NIGHTMARES!

My intention was to write a new (well, actually, the first!) handbook on Win-Win.

According to Wikipedia[1], a handbook is a 'type of reference work, or other collection of instructions, that is intended to provide ready reference... designed to be easily consulted and provide quick answers in a certain area.'

My objectives for this handbook are to:
- Present overwhelming arguments for the broad business advantages and applications of Win-Win.
- Add a new dimension to the topic—the Win-Win-Win Pyramid—giving a more optimistic and comprehensive framework to Win-Win by the fleshing out of Mutual Wins.
- Demonstrate how Win-Win can be applied in virtually all businesses.
- Give actionable best practices and tips to make Win-Win outcomes more probable and more achievable.

I hope that all of the above has been achieved.

In my introduction, I asked you to think about the Nightmare and refer back to it as you read through the book. If you recall, the Nightmare is your worst personal case study.

The one where you always stand to lose, or you have always lost. I suggested that it was probably the one that has given you sleepless nights and more stress than you would care for.

If you think back once again to the Nightmare, I hope that by now you have learnt something—a new Mutual Win, a different approach, an alternative perspective—that has helped you understand:

1. What you would have done differently.
2. What you will do differently in the future if faced with a similar scenario.

If this is the case, I trust that the money spent on the purchase of this book has been handsomely rewarded.

If this is not the case, I am sorry that this book has not helped. As I say, it was not my objective.

In putting the case studies together, I have reached out to a significant number of personal contacts from different business sectors, in different countries and in different roles.

As a fully paid-up member of the Win-Win Appreciation Society (if it were to exist!), I have been surprised at how many of these contacts informed me that, in their business field, there is only Win-Lose.

Without calling into question those businesses—or my contacts who operate in those fields—I have understood that Win-Win is sadly not universal, despite the positive aspects that I advanced in Chapter 1.4. There are inevitably Nightmare examples where Win-Win, and what we have learnt in this book, might not work... yet.

More encouragingly, I also had one contact who informed me that the industry he has worked in for the past 20 years has now moved from being entrenched in Win-Lose to being one in which industry protagonists now compete for competitive advantage via the scale of the Mutual Wins that they offer their customers! An industry that openly competes on Win-Win! Fantastic.

The thread that links all of these real-life case studies provided by my personal contacts is *pride*.

Finding a Win-Win solution, based on Mutual Wins, is by and large *not* the easy option to take. Nor is it the easy negotiation to make. That means that when the effort is made and the Win is achieved, the overriding emotion is justifiably one of pride. In all cases, there is pride that the better solution—for all parties, not just oneself—has been found.

Business fortunes change.

I am not referring to having a good/bad day or a good/bad negotiation. Here I refer to the long-term trajectory of every business.

Business trajectories changes.

Knowing the precise trajectory of your business each day is an almost impossible task. Businesses tend not to be motorboats that can move from one location to another or one speed to another in a simple matter of seconds. Instead, they are more like container ships, where changing direction and accelerating away are slow, time-consuming and (more) challenging tasks.

It is important for you to know, at least, if your business is heading in a positive, or negative, direction.

Positive in the sense that your business is winning more than losing. That there is a positive momentum around the business; in your team; with your customer; ideally, in your market. It's as if you are caught in a virtuous circle.

Negative means that none of the above apply. Here the danger is that of a vicious circle.

If it is positive, business actions should be taken to keep the business moving in this positive direction, to stay in a virtuous circle.

If it is negative, business actions must be taken remedy the situation, get the business back in the right direction and, above all, avoid moving into a vicious circle.

The business actions and decisions that are required daily in these two conflicting circles are, in my experience, completely different. With different time scales and deliverables, too...

Having run businesses in both vicious and virtuous circles, I find that managing the different challenges leads to very, very different professional experiences. They require and generate different emotions, too. Having common business tools and processes that help surmount these challenges and accompany you as a leader is extremely important.

The polyvalence and positive intentions of Win-Win make it a must-have addition to the decision-making kit bag.

Trajectories change. The issue is, how fast? 'The speed of change is accelerating,' says Mark Benioff[2], CEO of Salesforce. 'Companies are no longer competing against each other. They are competing with speed.' This is so true. There is no time to lose. Take Win-Win out of your kit bag today, and ask yourself how it can support change for the positive.

But watch out! If you don't, one of your competitors might be doing it! That cannot be positive for you.

Need any more convincing?

We have seen how versatile Win-Win is.

We have seen how Win-Win can help achieve negotiation outcomes that seemed out of reach at a first glance.

We have seen how the Win-Win-Win Pyramid can add a new Mutual Win dimension that might (just might) allow better opportunities and options to be examined. If this new tool will help one business, perhaps your business, move from a bad to a good trajectory, or a good to a better trajectory, then there can be no finer accolade.

Win-Win is not a guarantee of winning. That cannot be guaranteed. Nevertheless, I hope that you too are now a fully paid-up member of the Win-Win Appreciation

Society(!), and that you too believe the Win-Win-Win Pyramid can support you in implementing Win-Win in the future. Together they are guaranteed to bring you a greater chance of winning.

Let there be no more Nightmares.

ABOUT THE AUTHOR

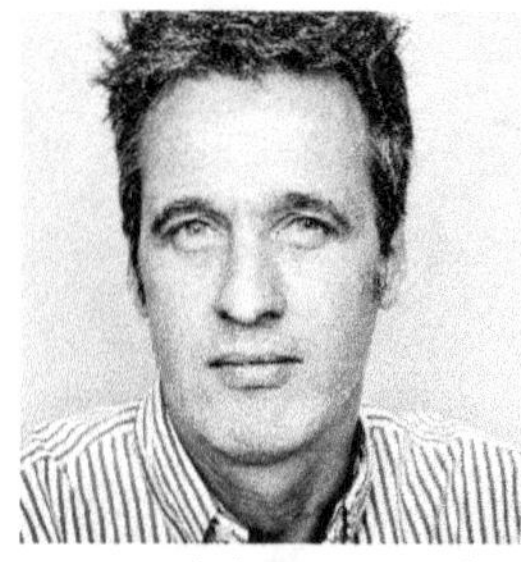

Philip Waterhouse is, among other things, the founder of the BRAVADO Group, specialists in leadership skills training. He previously spent more than 30 years working across four continents for L'Oréal, Hasbro and Triumph International, all market leaders in their respective fields. For the past 20 years, Philip has held general-management roles with national and international responsibilities, involving turnaround, business transformation and global brand reset projects.

British-born, he has lived outside the UK for most of the last 25 years. He currently lives in France with his wife, Valérie, and three children.

For better or for worse, he still supports England!

If you would like to get in touch, or learn more,
please contact the team at
philip.waterhouse@win-win-win.eu
or visit *www.win-win-win.eu.*

ENDNOTES

INTRODUCTION

1. http://purchasingnegotiationtraining.com/negotiation/what-does-win-win-negotiation-mean, Robert Menard (2009)

2. https://www.meetconstance.com/blog/2017/4/2/habit-4-think-win-win, Angela Duckworth (2017)

3. https://informaconnect.com/creating-a-win-win-strategy-during-a-negotiation, Sean Sydney (2019)

4. https://www.forbes.com/sites/rajshreeagarwal/2019/10/09/with-whom-should-you-trade-three-steps-to-win-win, Rajshree Agarwal (2019)

5. https://www.slideshare.net/IMechE/attitude-and-understanding-the-surprising-ways-you-can-improve-your-negotiation-skills, Institute of Mechanical Engineers (2015)

CHAPTER 1.1

1. John Stacey, 'Seven Examples of Win-Win', 15 April 2018. https://simplicable.com/new/lose-lose-situation

2. 'Welcome to Lafayette Morehouse', Lafayette Morehouse. Retrieved 1 June 2018.

3. https://sevenhabitsofhighlyeffectiveteensjameiamitchell.wordpress.com/2015/08/02/habit-4-think-win-win

4. You Can't Always Get What You Want © Abkco Music, Inc, Sony/ATV Music Publishing LLC, Keith Richards /Mick Jagger.

CHAPTER 1.2

1. https://www.goodreads.com/quotes/325957-dieting

CHAPTER 1.4

1. *The 7 Habits of Highly Effective People: Powerful Lessons in Personal Change Interactive Edition*, p.255, Mango Media Inc, Stephen R. Covey (2016).

CHAPTER 2.1

1. https://www.brainyquote.com/quotes/jimmy_carter_140962#

CHAPTER 2.2

1. For the benefit of the P&L cost-block exercise, I have included commercial discounts below the turnover line to demonstrate the impact on P&L when additional discount is given. In such cases, turnover is often stated in two P&L lines: (i) turnover at list price (i.e. turnover based on the catalogue product prices without any discounts), and (ii) net turnover (i.e. once all commercial discounts and other customer commercial conditions are taken into consideration)
2. *Futureproof: How to Get Your Business Ready for the Next Disruption*, p. xxx, FT Publishing, Minter Dial and Caleb Storkey (2017)

CHAPTER 2.6

1. https://en.wikipedia.org/wiki/Category_management

CHAPTER 2.7

1. https://corporatefinanceinstitute.com/resources/knowledge/deals/what-is-batna

CHAPTER 4.1

1. https://en.wikipedia.org/wiki/Handbook
2. http://marketingcloud.com/blog35-digital-marketing-quotes-to-memorize-and tweet/ Marc Benioff, CEO Salesforce (2014)

9 782957 770007